My Adventure to the New World

My Adventure to the New World

A real life story of a Vietnamese American

Paul Nguyen

River Breeze Publishing

My Adventure to the New World .

River Breeze Publising
www.riverbreezepublishing.com
orders@riverbreezepublishing.com

Copyright © 2014 by Paul Nguyen.

All rights reserved. No other part of this book may be reproduced, stored in a retrival system, or transmitted in any form or by any electronic or mechanical means without the prior written permission of the publisher. The only exception is brief quotations in printed reviews.

Print in the United States of America
First Edition 2014.

My Adventure to the new World / by Paul Nguyen.
A real life story of a Vietnamese American

ISBN 978-0-9916035-0-3

Library of Congress Control Number: 2014905499

To the parents who had sacrificed so much for their children and all the kind and loving people who had helped us, the refugees, during the toughest times of our lives.

Contents

	Prologue	9
1.	The Incident at Sea	19
2.	My Early Childhood	27
3.	The Vietnam War	39
4.	The First Wave of Bombard	45
5.	The Play Ground	51
6.	Running Away from Home	63
7.	My Father	69
8.	The First Sea Travel	83
9.	My Mother	97
10.	The Second Wave of Bombard	113
11.	Life in The Countryside	129
12.	Return to City	145
13.	The New Business	169
14.	The Vietnam China War	179
15.	The First Escape	185
16.	The First Love	199

My Adventure to The New World

17. The Second Escape   215
18. The Long Sea Journey   225
19. Arriving to Hong Kong   265
20. Life in The Refugee Camp 281

Prologue

Time is flying by so fast. It feels just as a flash of time and it has been so many years passing by. There is an old saying that a human life is compared to the horse steps passing by our door. Recalling the fond childhood time when we were living with our parents and those times listening to the legendary stories that our parents were telling us, we all would treasure those lovely memories in our lives. Those bed time stories had been educational and sometimes very interesting. Some of the fairy tales had special meaning and had helped developing our imagination during the growing up of our childhood. I recall one of the stories was so fascinating that it still stays with me to today.

The story was about the meeting of a young man with his loving fairy. Long time ago, in the reign of the Tran family in Vietnam under the king Quang Thai (1388-1398), there was a young man born at Hoa Chau Village, Tien Du District. (The district is now called Bac Ninh City in present time). The young man's name was Tu Thuc and he was from a noble family. When he was in his early adulthood, he was promoted into a low rank mandarin in his district. But he had loved to travel around the country enjoying the nature and writing his own poems more than his work.

In nearby his home district, there was a famous Buddhism temple and in front of the temple was a very beautiful flower garden. In this garden grew a rare and strange peony flower plan, and every year at the blooming period, around February, people arranged a jubilant festival to attend the beyond price flowers. The festival time had been a special time for boys and girls to meet each other and becoming lovers. (There is some rumor that this temple is the Phat Tich Temple at Bac Ning today).

One day in February of 1396 and during the festival time, people saw a strange young beautiful girl about fifteen years old attending the festival. She did not wear any make up but her skin was smooth and radiant as the fresh flower pedal. She came close to the spe-

Prologue

cial flower and pulled in the branch to smell its pleasant fragrance, and by accident, broke the slender branch. The flower was the main reason people came and donated their money to the temple; therefore, some lay brothers at the temple detained her for the ransom.

Tu Thuc also came to visit the famous temple that day and saw the incident. He did not bring enough money with him that day so he took off his very expensive coat and gave to the lay brothers to redeem the young girl. The girl was released and appreciated for the kindness of Tu Thuc. She thanked him, walked off and disappeared in the crowd.

Tu Thuc had been known for his kind ness and generosity, after the incident at the temple, he was loved even more by the people in his village. But Tu Thuc was more a romantic person than a person of work. He loved wine, poet, and often travelled away from his home. He was reprimanded one time for his work neglecting by the higher officer. The higher authority offical said to him that his father had been a very successful high ranking mandarin and he should be able to handle his lower rank position better than his father. Tu Thuc exclaimed to himself: "Oh Heaven! Is it for just several rice bushels and I have to bury myself in this place? Why not resign from this position and wandering with the beloved nature to enjoy all the beauties of this lifetime!" He returned his official seal, resigned and then moved to Tong Son, a district of magnificent landscape and scenic places with many majestic mountains and caves. His footmark and poem verses were imprinted all over Chich Tro Mountain, Luc Van Cave, Le River, Kenh Nga Trail...

One day he travelled farther to Than Phu Sea (Divine Light Sea) and saw a five-color cloud appeared from a distance. He rented a small boat from a native boatman and travelled into the area. When he got there, he saw many very strange lofty mountains and brooks. He was agitated by the majestic landscape and said to the boatman: "I have travelled many places but never see or heard of this unreal beautiful and strange place." In a whim, a new poem came to his mind. He asked the boatman to tie his boat and waited for him while he went into a large cave to write his new poem onto a cliff. He was walking into the open of the cave and suddenly a large cloud covered all over him that he could not see anything around him. Then he heard the sound of some brook from a distance. He traced the sound of the brook and leaned on the cliff to walk toward the pleasant sound. The interstice was getting brighter and he was able to see the tunnel gradually expending. Then out of the darkness, his eyes were dazzled with the bright light again. He was overwhelmed with many colorful of the spectacular gardens full of flowers ahead. The very unusual and pleasant scent from the flowers gave him the feeling of ecstasy. There were a few temples and palaces covered by colorful jewelry flickering out from afar.

He was still in ecstasy and thought he was in a dream but then he heard a soft but clear laughter from someone nearby. He turned and saw two young girls were giggling and saying to each other: "Behold, the new groom is coming!" and then walked away and disappeared into the garden. He was still in astonishing but then the girls came back out from the garden and said to him politely: "Our lady invites you to our palace". He followed the girls, walking on the walkway embroiled with so many colorful flowers, toward their palace. After a decent distance of walk, he heard vaguely the sound of some soft music coming out from the palace. The pleasant music was clearer and clearer and then a whole splendid palace appeared in sight. Above the gate was a large horizontal lacquered board with golden row of letters "GIAO QUANG DIEN" (Light Crossing Palace) engraved on it.

Inside the palace, a fairy dressed in bright white dress was waiting for him. She greeted him and then said: "You are a kind man enthralled with a strong love for the nature. Do you know where this palace is?"

Tu Thuc nervously replied: "I am just a reclusive scholar of Tong Son district. My heart is infected with only earthly knowledge. I was wandering about to contemplate the nature and was intrigued by the strange and beautiful mountains and wanted to explore the area. Please let me know where I am so my earthly mind would be clearer".

The woman said softly: "Right! How could you know this place! This is the sixth in thirty six of Phi Lai Cung (Heaven Coming Oasis). This whole place is an oasis hovering off the ground as the La Phu Mountain (Low Hovering Mountain) appears and disappears with the wind, as the Bong Lai Summit (Floating Coming Summit) rising above the waves. I am the owner of the Light Crossing Palace. I know you are a kind young man so I invited you here." The fairy lady turned and signaled to the girl standing nearby. The girl came inside, and in a short moment, a beautiful young girl in light blue dress came out. Tu Thuc recognized immediately that was the very girl who had broken the flower branch in the Buddhism temple at the previous festival.

The gorgeous girl's name was Giang Huong (Descending Fragrance) and she had been deeply moved by Tu Thuc's help saving her from the incident at the temple and had fallen in love with him since. She has been unhappy after leaving him at the temple and wanted to see him again. Her mother could not do anything to make her happy except to invite Tu Thuc to this place. Right after the rejoining of the young couple, the wedding ceremony was performed for both of them and Tu Thuc stayed back at the palace.

Living happily with Giang Huong for almost a year, Tu Thuc started to feel the sadness of nostalgia. One day when they were with each other, he told Giang Huong: "I have been away from home for a long time and sometimes felt homesick. I want to go back to visit my family". Giang Houng sadly replied: "I am not a narrow-minded person and trying to keep you around me all the time. But Earthly life is very short. I am afraid that when you get back there, everything has changed so much beyond your recognition."

After that she arranged a special chariot for him to go. She also gave him a sealed letter and told him: " Go and visit your family. Open this letter only when when you are really missing me."

Tu Thuc said good-bye to everyone in the palace, and in just a blink, he was at Tong Son Mountain in his home district. He went into his village and looked for his home but everything was very different. Except for the mountains and the river in the village were not changed and he could recognize them, all village houses were beyond his recognition. He asked the old people in the village and one old man said: "When I was young I had heard that back to the last fourth generation of our ancestors there was a man also named Tu Thuc. But he has been lost in some wilderness almost two hundred years ago".

Tu Thuc was very sad. He came back to Tong Son Mountain but his chariot had disappeared. He opened the letter of Giang Huong and she wrote: "On Light Crossing Palace married. Our providence had ended. It is extremely hard to find Heaven Coming Oasis again!" Tu Thuc realized then that the letter was her final farewells.

Afterward, one day some village people saw Tu Thuc, dressed in fur-coat and light hat, alone went into Hoanh Son mountain chain (Horizon Mountain Chain) and never come back out.

In most of the other similar stories about life in another unseen realm, time was slow and very much different from our earthly space-time. Which should give us all the sense of appreciation for our mundane life on this Earth. In just a blink of time at the other realms, here on Earth we could do so many different things and went through of lot of experience with our lives. Our earthly life here must have some special meaning and perhaps a specific purpose for each one of us.

As an immigrant to this new country, I have met many refugee people during the journey of my own refugee life and have listened to many whimsical life stories of different people. Some of those stories had driven me into tears. Many of those people have settled to the new world and are still struggling with their daily adjustment to the new life style. Some had adjusted well, be assimilated, and are very happy, but many were having a feeling of being isolated and still missing their former life style. However, most of the immigrant people would express that they would be willing to sacrifice their own lives for the better of their children's futures if they have to do it all over again. I have also met many American people and have been asked many questions such as "Where are you from? Why you are here? How did you get to America?"…

With humble thoughts, I would like to narrate an interesting real life story of a friend of mine which I had been told a few years ago, hoping that with my trivial story telling ability and mediocre writing skill, I will be able to entertain you the readers for a few hours of your spare time. The story would also introduce the reader to the life of a typical family in a small country at the other half of our mother Earth.

1. The Incident at Sea

The boat was sailing with a moderate speed over the peaceful ocean not too far from the shoreline. As usual, I was sitting with my brother and some other men at the open area near the front section of the boat. The weather was nice and clear with the cool breeze blowing gently over the vast open ocean space. The red sun was gradually emerging out from the horizon. With the dim sunlight one could see the silhouettes of a couple other sail-boats scattering out at sea from afar. Looking toward land from the left side of the boat was the dimly view of the accumulated-mountain-landscape. As in any other morning, the boat owner boiled some water to prepare the morning tea for him and a few other men on-board. Some women had woken up earlier and were preparing their daily activities too. I am not into tea that much, but just coming out from a cold, I wasn't feeling well that day, so I asked the man for a small cup of hot tea to waken up my not fully awake mind at that time. Dawn is the most peaceful time out at sea and has the prettiest oceanic scenery in the whole day.

The sun was rising a little higher and the view of the far landscape was getting a little clearer. But the signs of the other sail boats were getting smaller and smaller as those boats were moving away from land. Perhaps the people on those boats were on their ways to the deep ocean fishing. While a few people on-board were having some tea and chatting with one another, suddenly we felt a strange vibration in the boat. Everyone was startled and flabbergasted, stared at each other, but no one knows right away what had happened. I once before had seen a huge fish protruding out of the ocean surface so a thought that a large fish had hit some area underneath the boat came to my mind. The boat was still moving and people were getting back to enjoy their tea and their conversation. Right at that moment, one person sitting by the front helm probably heard the sound of running water. He bent close to the boat floor as he was trying to listen close to the mysterious sound. Then he stood up immediately and with a panicked manner, he yelled:

"Aqueous rock, aqueous rock, the boat had hit the aqueous rock!!!"

The helm in the front part of the boat had hit the aqueous rock at the bottom of the ocean. Water was running into the bottom of the boat silently and the boat was gradually sinking. Everybody stood up in dismay but was still stunned by the incident. One young man, who has been taught by the helm man and knew a little about sailing by that time, heard the yelling. He ran out from the inside section of the boat and immediately pulled up the helm. The helm was stuck at the slot so another nearby person jumped in to give the young man a hand. With two persons, they were able to pull the helm out of the slot. But that did not stop the water from pouring into the boat; that might only prevent the boat from any farther hitting. The distance from the boat to the land was too far for anyone on the boat to swim to. There were pregnant woman and children on-board. A few persons were looking around in bewilderment and were searching for which part of the boat they should cling on. One person cried aloud: "help! help! help!" toward the Chinese boats from the very far distance hoping that someone on those boats might hear him. More women came out from the inside area to the side of the boat; they all were waving their hand toward the other boats and calling out for help. They forgot that they themselves could not see those boats clearly. The distance was too far. No one on those boats could see them or hear their help call either!

The helm person sitting by the rudder at the far back of the boat, left the ruder and ran quickly into the living section of the boat while calling out for someone else to hold the rudder for him. He removed the plank wood cover of the store space underneath and looked down. Two other men and I followed him into the boat and looked down to the store space. A lot of water had filled about half the space down there inside the boat and the water level seemed rising fast. The helm person quickly asked for an empty bucket and started drawing out the water underneath as fast as he could. Another man helped him dumped the water in the bucket back to sea. A few other men came in and were ready for any helping hand. By scooping out the water quickly, the water level underneath the boat floor was not rising as fast as before and the boat was still able to move slowly over the water surface. The helm person gave the bucket back to another man to draw out the water for him and ran back to the back of the boat to control the rudder and steered the boat toward land.

Then the person who had pulled up the front helm crawled into the under space and

The Incident at Sea

into the water at the bottom of the boat; with the help of a little sunlight shining through the opening, he recognized the water was coming at the area next to the slot of the front helm. He called out for a thick blanket. Another man immediately crawled in there with a blanket and they both pressed the folded blanket down tightly at the cracked area. The water was still coming in but not as rapid as before. Another person crawled in and squeezed down another smaller blanket at the crevice. After a short moment, we were able to control the seawater level inside the boat and the boat was moving a little faster toward land.

With a large plastic bucket, we continued drawing out the water quickly and enough to prevent the boat from sinking down any deeper. The distance to the shore was getting closer and closer. By then people standing around knew we were out of the dangerous moment and felt a little less panicky. Everyone sighed out with relief.

Once the boat got close at the beach, a few men jumped out and pulled the boat onto the shore. Then everyone got off the boat and helped pushing the boat onto the sand floor. The crevice at the front section of the boat was finally raised above the water surface and water stopped coming into the boat. People tied the boat down to the beach floor with the anchor rope and drew out the rest of the sea water inside the boat. The boat was parked part on sand floor and part in the water.

Although we had not known the terrain well and had let the boat hitting the aqueous rock, it was very fortunate that the boat had been moving slower than usual and had not hit the rock too hard. We were also lucky that one person was sitting right by the helm at the time the boat hit the aqueous rock and that person had recognized the situation soon enough. More than that the incident had happened during daytime with enough daylight for people to detect the collided spot before the boat had been filled with too much seawater. The boat could have been sunken and we would have been drowned without any of the above facts. We all thanked Heaven that our lives were saved.

After setting the boat firmly to the sand floor, people looked around the place for any sight of people living around but that place was just a bare beach area behind the dense woods and some rocky mountains. There was no sign of resident housing or anybody living nearby. The silhouettes of a couple of other boats out at sea had also disappeared off into the horizon. We had just barely breathed out and released from the panic, but again were confronted with another dilemma: how to fix the boat in the middle of nowhere. People were wondering if we would be able to go on with our journey or all of us would become jungle people in this wild place.

Most of us were so tired after the incident, sat down on the sand floor around the boat to rest. I also lay my back down and looked up the sky with different thoughts coming into my mind: The food and fresh water we had might not be enough for all of us in a few more days. There was not any hunting or fishing equipment on-board. We all had evaded death from all the drastic bombards of warfare and other severe ordeals to be stuck in this desert land? It would not make any sense for us to be starved in this place! But I was exhausted at that moment; I closed my eyes and recalled all the experiences that I had gone through with my life.

My Adventure to The New World

2. My Early Childhood

I was born in the Vietnam War and grew up during the toughest economic period of North Vietnam. My family lived in Haiphong, a major port city and is the second largest city of North Vietnam behind Hanoi, the country's capital. I was the youngest boy in a family of four brothers and two sisters. Back to the time I was about seven or eight years old and could remember clearly, my two brothers were still teenagers and were attending high school in the city; one of my sisters was still in the middle school. I was in the first grade and was home schooling then. We all lived together with our parents in the second floor of a town house located in the middle of a short cross street between the two rivers. The Tam Bac River was running along the side of one of the main streets two blocks from the left side of my house, and the Lap River was at about the same distance from my house by the right side.

Despite the tough economic condition of ours and most other families in the neighborhood at the time, those were the lovely and dreamy days of my fond childhood. Everymorning, my brothers and sister were attending school until noon, so I was the only one left at home with my mother and sometimes helped her with the sundry house-chores. My daily chores were sweeping the house and cleaning the tea set in the morning, and once every few days, I had to wipe the tile floor of the house with a bucket of water and a wiping cloth for my mother wanted to keep our house very clean. By nine o'clock I would start up the charcoal cooking-stove and got it ready for my mother to cook our meals. I sometimes help my mom preparing and cleaning the cooking materials and equipments for her. In Vietnam, people usually cook separate lunch and dinner and would eat together at home. My mom often went to the local market twice a day, once in the morning and once in the afternoon, to buy the comestibles so they could be fresher because we did not have refrigerator back then. When she bought them back, I would help clean them for her.

When our lunch was ready, my mom would prepare the lunch box and gave it to me to deliver it to my father while he was at work. My father worked in a factory on the other side of the Tam Bac River not too far from our house. Around eleventh o'clock on every working day, Monday to Saturday, was my lunch delivering time. I would take my father's lunch box and walk across the suspension bridge by the Tam Bac River on my way to his factory.

Walking on the rope bridge would give one a feeling of freedom but with a little cautious. The bridge was old and not welled maintained and there were holes on it as some of the planks on the surface of the bridge were missing. People had to be very careful with their foot steps while walking on the bridge other wise they would take a false step into the hole and might fall into the river. Most of the times I would stop and took my time on the bridge to enjoy the cool breeze of the river and to observe other people's activities around that area.

On the main street by the riverside away from the bridge area, people stacked bags of material which were unloaded from the transporting boats into many high mounds of bags on top of each other. Young boys often came there to play the fighting game or hide-and-seek on or around those mounds. Once in a while, some boats full of spice bags were uploaded onto the brink of the river. Sometimes the workers carried large bags of cinnamon barks up from the boat and a lot of cinnamon barks were scattered at the dock. The boys took the scattered barks home and they would eat them raw. Some older boys even cut the bark into small pieces and rolled them into a cigarette to smoke. The raw cinnamon has a spicy and sweet taste that the naive boys seemed to enjoy. But by consuming too much raw cinnamon many boys in my neighborhood had been affected seriously with constipating, nosebleed problems and sometimes even urinating out with blood.

During the Summer time when the water level of the river was high, the children often gathered at the dock or the bridge to swim. It was fun to see them standing on the edge of the dock and jumped down to the river as they were playing with one another. But sometimes a few boys gathered at the bridge and climbed high up on the wire-rope of the suspension bridge. They waited until some young girl passing by and jumped down to the river water. The water would splash all over the bridge surface and the body of the poor girl passing by. Every year there would be at least one person drowned at that river section. People in my neighborhood said that the river had a curse at that area but it did not scare away the pesky boys.

Standing on the bridge near the river bank area on low tide days one could see a lot of the little crabs living at the river banks. The cute little crab had a huge red claw on one side and a very tiny one the other side. Without their huge colorful claws, it would be very hard to detect them from the muddy surface. Sometimes there were a few boys hanging around the side of the river and from time to time they would go down to the bank to catch the crabs. The boys used the long strings and made a loop at the end on the strings. As the boys got down to the bank, all the little crabs would run quickly into the little holes on the ground. The river bank at that section became a animated view of a lot of the swiftly moving little red dots on the ground. The banks turned back into a quiet ground with its muddy color once all the crabs were inside those small holes. The boys would set the loops at the end of the strings around the holes and went back to the side of the river and waited there while holding the other ends of the strings. After a short quiet moment, the crabs would slowly come out of the holes. When the crabs just showed up at the end of the holes, the boys pulled the strings quickly. The little crabs were either tied by the loop at the end of strings or flew to the side of the river. The flying crabs were caught quickly by the fast hands of the energetic boys before they could run back to the river bank.

As a sign that heralded what would happen to me later on with my life, I had always been attracted by the boats that berthing at the river. Every time passing by, I was very curious about how the whole family of the fishermen could live inside just a small boat. The fishermen had their own wood stove at the back of their boat and cooked their meals there. Standing on the bridge, one could look into part of their living area inside their boat. The living space inside the boat was so small that they always had to stoop their body very low while moving around the inside area. The smoke from their wood stoves and the smell of their cooked foods emitted around the area created a peaceful and lively scenery in this place.

Sometimes the river water was quiet and clear, one could see many schools of small fishes gathering at some pieces of the food scraps floating on the water surface. From time to time, there was a fisherman standing by the dock to fish using his hoof lift net. Most of the times, the fisher man could only capture the small fishes. But one time I saw a fisher man captured a large fish the size of an adult salmon. The fisherman was so happy that day; he stopped his fishing and ran to the nearby fish market to sell his fish right away.

Seeing so many fishes in the river always caused me wanting to go fishing. I remember one time I really wanted to go fishing but did not have the money to buy any fishing equipment and had to make up my own fishing gear. The fishing hook was created from a small piece of the bicycle brake wire. The fishing line was from some of the strong thread in my mother sewing box. The fishing rod was a piece of bamboo branch, and the bait was the flies which could be caught near some trash on any street. A piece of a cock's tail feather was tied to the fishing line as the float to hold up the baited end of the fishing line. Without asking for the consent of my mother, I came to the river and sat alone quietly on a large concrete bar under the dock where a lot of small fishes often appeared. That was my first time fishing at the river. It was a very hot sunny day but fishing in this quiet hidden spot was very cool and comfortable. The river breeze blew gently under the space of the dock created an ideal place to fish. I just sat there and enjoyed the secretive feeling of my first fishing with my unique fishing rode in hand.

In just short moment, I notice the fishing float was pulled down slightly, and then it went all the way down. I pulled my rod and felt the poor fish fighting at the end of the line.

My Adventure to The New World

I was so excited; with both hands, I lifted the rod and got a small fish the size of my hand. I ran home with the rod and the fish still being hooked in the line. Could not hide my joy, I showed the fish to my mother that day. She reprimanded me for doing it without asking her permission; however, seeing me so happy and did not want to ruin my success; she cleaned and fried that fish for me to eat at our dinner that day. The first fish I caught by my own hand was a small fish of mediocre quality, but it seamed to taste much better than any other fishes that I had ever eaten before.

Later that day, my father found out about my fishing activity and he forbade me from playing near the river. He said that according to my horoscope, before my teenage years and especially at the age of twelve, I might drown if I play near the water. Since that day, delivering my father's lunch was the only time I was allowed to come by this place. Every time I delivered my father's lunch, I would take time marooning at the area to enjoy the feeling of the free spirit of the beloved river.

Home schooling was hard for anyone to have friends. Also, for the safety reason, my mother didn't want me to play outside on the streets with other boys. There was no toy available those days, so for entertainment, the boys at our neighborhood usually played a very rough fighting game. More than that, the boys sometimes used obscene language with each other. Therefore, my mother always tried to keep me inside. Many times I was bored and had wished to have some toys to play with.

One time on the way to deliver my father's lunch, I heard the sound of a little bird at the tree nearby, I came closer to the tree and saw a little sparrow on the ground. The tiny bird exposed its bare pinkish skin on its body as it was too young and had not had enough feathers to cover its entire body yet. Perhaps the bird had been fallen down from its nest on the tree by accident. It could not even move as I came and picked it up. Luckily it fell on the thick grass on the ground and was not serious injured. I took the bird home with me. I found a small carton box and put some hay inside it. I cut a small hole on the box's lid, put the little bird in side the box and closed the lid. The little bird was tired and needed to rest. I set the box inside the dish-cabinet at my backyard and closed the door of the cabinet behind me.

After a long moment, I came back to the disk-cabinet to check on the bird, the little bird had recuperated its strength and seamed very hungry. It chirped repeatedly and its beak wide opened every time my hand was getting close to the box. I rolled some cooked rice into a small ball and put inside its beak. The little bird swallowed the whole thing down right away. I repeated a few times until the bird was full and did not open its beak anymore. I did not forget to deepen my finger into a cup of water and let my wet finger touching the beak of the little bird after each time I fed it so the bird could drink down the dripping water from my finger. After feeding it, I would put the bird back into the disk-cabinet.

As I was helping my mother at the kitchen and sometimes passing by the cabinet, the bird heard my foot steps and chirped repeatedly as it was trying to get my attention. The bird grew healthily. In just a few days, its feathers had covered its entire body. It fluttered its wings every time I removed the lid of its box. It really brought me so much joy to see the lovely bird responding to me as I was its very own mother. Even though it was not able to fly yet, after a few more days the little bird could hop small steps on the ground. When I set the bird down on the floor, sitting a few steps away and whistled, the little bird would flutter its wings and hop to me. It was a joyful feeling to have a little friend following me around my house.

The bird kept me entertained and I could play with it all day. I carried the little bird with me inside the pocket of my shirt almost all the time. After a few weeks from the time I took the bird home, the bird was gradually able to fly a short distance. Every time when I wanted to feed it, I set the bird at a distance and whistled, the bird could fly to me and alighted on my chest. The claws of the little bird grasped firmly on my shirt and into my skin. I could feel the warmness of its body leaning on me. That made us so close to each other and gave me a special feeling as my feeble friend was totally depended on me for its protection. The distance the bird could fly was getting longer each day. I loved my bird so much and afraid that I might loose it, I just played with the bird inside my house then. I once had thought about cutting the feathers of its wings shorter so it would not fly away from me.

One day I was playing at the balcony of my house, I saw many wild sparrows playing on the roof of the house at the opposite street. There was a young wild sparrow just like the one I had. That young sparrow was chattering as it followed other older birds around that roof area. The little bird seemed very happy living together with its own group in their natural habitat. My little sparrow came to my mind. It must be much happier for my little bird to live with its own family. Even though the bird was my only friend and I loved it so much, I decided to bring it back to its family.

The next day, I put the bird inside the chest pocket of my shirt and took the bird with

My Adventure to The New World

me on my way to deliver my father's lunch. When I got to the tree that I had found the bird, I set it on a small branch and went on to my father factory. At the factory, as I sat waiting for my father to finish his lunch, I could not keep my mind away from the tree that I had set my bird; I was anxious and hoping to see my bird again. When my father finished his lunch, I took the empty lunch box and hurriedly ran back there. When I got back to the tree, the bird was no longer at that place; perhaps it had found its follow-creatures and had followed other birds away.

I felt sadly such as an old friend had let me down and would never coming back to me. Without my little friendly bird, the day seamed long and boring. Sometimes I just stood at the balcony of my house and watched the wild sparrows playing at the roof of the opposite house. All the sparrows looked the same; I wondered if my little friend was one among those little creatures.

3. The Vietnam War

On September 2nd 1954, the Declaration of Independence of Democratic of Vietnam was announced by Ho Chi Minh in Ba Dinh, Hanoi. After the victory of the Vietnamese people against the French at the Siege of Dien Bien Phu, the French colonial administration in Vietnam ended and Vietnam was dissolved under the Geneva Accords of 1954, which separated the forces of the former French supporters and the communist nationalists at the 17th parallel north with the Vietnamese Demilitarized Zone. A 300-day period of free movement was given for all Vietnamese people to choose which side to reside. The partition of Vietnam, with Ho Chi Minh's Democratic Republic of Vietnam in North Vietnam, and Emperor Bao Dai's State of Vietnam in South Vietnam, was not intended to be permanent by the Geneva Accords, and the Accords expressly forbade the interference of third powers. However, in 1955, the State of Vietnam's Prime Minister, organized a referendum to topple Bao Dai and proclaimed himself president of the Republic of Vietnam. Vietnam was officially divided into two separated regions with two different governments.

Determined to unite the country, the newly formed North Vietnamese Government had taken time to gather all its available resources and man power for its political ambition and preparing its armed forces to take over the South.

I remember during my early childhood, I once heard on the radio the voice of Ho Chi Minh, the president of North Vietnam at the time announced that "The country of Vietnam is one, the people of Vietnam is one, the rivers may dried out, the mountains may wore off, but that true will never changed." At that time I was young and so naïve that I did not even understand that Vietnam had two separated governments. The land of Vietnam is not large, but it incorporates over 50 ethnic groups. Except for the Kinh or Viet people living throughout the country's plains and occupying the majority, others find their places on the hill and the mountainous areas and are preserving their very own cultures and dressing patterns. Our home was close to the China Town and I had seen many Chinese Nationals and other ethnic minority people in my home town so I was assuming that our president was talking about the different ethnic groups living inside the country.

However, I was old enough to notice that people in our neighborhood were having a very destitute life. Under the communism system, the government controlled everything. Private business in any noticeable scale could be considered by the government as a crime of the people. No one has been allowed to produce or to sell anything in private. If anyone had any business idea and wanted to start a business, that person must get the permission from the local authority to set up a co-operative society and the authority would censor all the business activities and any profit of their business. Sometimes, the government would unexpectedly search the home of any family they had suspected and could confiscate all their properties. That was one of the main reasons that most people were reluctant to work hard then.

Except some manufacturing plants left behind from the French colonial era, the whole industrial system of the country was so poor and produced almost nothing. The only products North Vietnam could make were some simple machine components for the contracts of the foreign companies oversea. In the factories and work-shops, the salaries for the workers were little and about the same for every worker regardless of how productive they were. People called these salaries "starvation wages". The salaries were usually not nough to support the people's family daily living. In the factories and work-shops, the workers just showed up at work mainly to get their paychecks at the end of each month and the pace of work at any factory or work-shop was very slow. Most of the workers usually took a long rest during their break times and would sit together in some small tea-shops near the outside of the gate areas of the factories to chat or to joke with one another. They seemed not worrying much about being fired by their bosses; they were only concerned about how they would steal some raw material of the factories home to sell it in the black market for some extra money to feed their families.

Vietnam is an agricultural country and more than eighty percent of the population were farmers at the time. The main food consumption of the Vietnamese is rice; however, North Vietnam did not produce enough rice for its people at the time. All the private lands had been confiscated and became public property. The farmers worked together at the public-own-land on the rice fields as the agricultural co-operative societies. They would get their shares at harvest time with the amount of rice depending on the number of people in their families; the rest would belong to the public property and was controlled by the authority. Therefore, the farmers had not have the real motivation to work hard and, as a result, the fields had not produced high yield either.

Trying to motivate people to work harder, in the factories, work-shops, and co-operative societies, the administrators now and then set up some kind of contest for the workers to emulate, but the winning price were usually some award certificates without any monetary value. People lost their interests and would not participate in any emulating contest anymore. The government officials had created a lot of banners with slogans and were hanging them all over the public areas, but no one was paying any attention to those slogans anymore. That had wasted even more money and materials for those silly things.

In the cities, each family was provided with a rice-quota book for buying rice from the public stores and some type of coupons for other comestible products. Most of the time in the cities, rice had been a shortage product and not enough to provide as in the quotas, at that time the public rice-stores would sell dried noodle, wheat flour, buckwheat, or corn in addition to rice. Other comestible products would be sold at the other different stores. The waiting lines at those stores were usually very long at the time the product was available. Meat and fish were some rare food products; if it was available, the buyers had to be there very early before it would run out. Sometimes people knew ahead that those rare products would be available at a certain store the next day, many people then would prepare to come to the store at 3 o'clock in the morning to wait with hope that they would be able to buy some meat for their family. Most of the common people were living in poverty with major nutrition deficiency condition at that time.

4. The First Wave of Bombard

After the administrator of North Vietnam had prepared its arm force, the North Vietnamese Army started to attack some of the cities of the South nearby the Vietnamese Demilitarized Zone. By that time, The United States of America had allied with South Vietnam to defend against the communism invasion from the North.

As the Vietnam War was getting more intense at the border between the North and the South, the American bombarders started the first wave of aerial bombard to the major cities of North Vietnam. The alarm siren on top of the tower of the water company in my city would go off to warn people when the radar detected the American bombarders were on their way the city, at that time, people would look for some nearby air-raid shelters for their protection. People would either jump down to the individual shelters in the ground, the zigzag trenches, or finding some places inside the building to hide from the flying debris during the bombing.

On the ground at the side walk of the streets, the city dug many individual shelters about five and half feet deep and four feet in diameter. They buried the concrete pipes of the same size of one and half inches thick into the holes. The top of the pipes were buried level with the ground and covered by two semicircle flaps of the same material. Each individual shelter would fit one or two persons inside. People would jump down and pulled the covers to close the buried pipes when they heard the alarm siren. At some large open ground areas such as in the parks, nearby the rivers, or even on some streets, the zigzag tunnels were dug down in the ground as another type of bunkers for a larger number of people. The tunnel was about four and a half feet wide, five and a half feet deep, and about forty feet long. The top of the tunnels were covered with concrete slaps and heaps of dust. The two ends of the tunnel were left open with stair steps for people to get in and out.

The town house my family living in was

a brick three-story duplex with red tile roof. The house was old and built simply as a rectangular box with three levels. Each level had two large adjoined rooms and each room was served as a living quarter for one family. The size for each living quarter was twelve feet wide and thirty feet long with an eighteen-feet-high ceiling approximately. There were six families living in the duplex. Two families were living on each level, one at each side. Behind the two living quarters on each level was a common open yard. Passing the common yards was the common kitchen room with door and window. Inside the area of the common yards from the ground level to the second floor was a strong concrete stairs. There was a large space under the concrete stairs and was used as a storage room. In the bombing periods, this storage room was used as a common hiding place during the bombarding. From the second level to the third level was only a light and smaller wooden stair. This whole town house had belonged to my family during the French colonial era. After the communism government took control of North Vietnam, the duplex was confiscated by the new government and became public property. The government had let five other families to share the whole town house with us. My family had been living on the second level in one side of the duplex since then.

When the alarm siren went off, people

in the building would run down and would get into the space under the concrete stairs, most of them were women and children. When I got down there during the air-raids, I usually found many people were already there. Sometimes, the hiding space under the stairs was packed with people. It was dark inside the area since all the lights must turn off to avoid the site detection of the bombing jets during the air-raids. It was difficult to see anyone's face clearly in there. I could only hear the mumbling of people praying in the darkness; some Christians, probably my mother and my sisters, were praying God to forgive their souls for knowing that we could die in any moment the bomb hit our building. Other Buddhism people were praying and asking Buddha to protect them. The more intense the aerial assault out on the air, the louder the praying sounds of the people inside the hiding place. Out side, the sounds of the flying jets and the air-defense artillery whizzing in the air intermingled with the busting of a few bombs at some distance now and then. Once in a while, the explosion of a nearby bomb vibrated the whole building. Sometimes at night time the hiding place was too crowded, some of us stood at the outside of the hiding place looking up to the sky through the open space over the stairs at our backyard. At that time the dark sky was lighted up with the red glares of the rockets and the anti-aircraft missiles firing up from the ground lighted up like a fiery web. The bombarding would stop in about five or ten minutes and the radio would announce that the bombing jets had left the city. People would return to their normal daily activities.

My father was still coming to work at the factory and I was delivering his lunch as usual. But since the time the city was under bombing attack, I was no longer able to enjoy the peaceful scenery of the river anymore. Every time passing the bridge, I must walk very fast instead of taking my time as I had usually done for I was so afraid that the jets would come and attack the bridge while I was walking on it.

After living with the bombing assault for a while, people seemed to get use to it and were not as afraid as in the beginning. A couple of times during the daytime, I stood with my brothers outside and watched the bombs dropping out from the bombing jet in the distance. At that time we could count the falling bombs in the air before the busting explosions on the ground. There was time the fighting jets were coming at night during our sleep and we were so tired and sleepy that we just kept on sleeping in our bed instead of running down stairs to the hiding place, thinking that we would die anyway if the bomb hit our building.

5. The Play Ground

At the time I was about eight years old, one day I was walking by a tropical fish store and saw a couple of male beta fishes in the small jars placing next to each other at the store window. The fishes were looking at each other through the jars and exerting their effort to fight. Their colorful fins spread out spectacularly which attracted my attention. I went inside the store and saw a large glass tank with many angel fishes of different sizes inside. The fish tank was decorated with a lot of water plants which turned the tank into a beautiful little aquatic world. I was captivated by the elegant beauty of a large pair of the angel fishes that always swam peacefully by each other. After gazing at them with veneration, I fell in love with the fishes and the tropical fish hobby started to occupy my mind.

After that day, I often came to that fish store to watch my favorite fishes. I could not take my eyes of the large spectacular fish tank with the angel fishes inside, but the angle fishes were too expensive and were not intended to be sold to kids. I only had some change so I bought the beta fish home. I put the fish in a large glass jar and placed a piece of broken mirror at the outside of the jar. Once the beta fish saw its image it would spread its bright blue beautiful fins widely to fight with its image. I was amazed and very entertained by the spectacular figure and aggressiveness of the fish, but I still loved the angel fishes more and wished that I would own a pair some day.

To feed my fish, I used a peace of copper wire, a bamboo branch, a piece of cloth to make my spoon-net. Everyday, I sneaked out the house with my spoon-net and an empty metal can and went to some of the zigzag trench or individual shelters that had stagnant rain water inside. There were a lot of mosquito larvae in the stagnant water. Using my spoon-net, I could skim the larvae out of the water and took them home in a can of water to feed my fish.

In those days, everyone in our family

often went to the cathedral to attend Mass. There were Masses everynight from Thursday to Sunday. There were usually three to four Masses on Sunday. The cathedral was not too far from our home and we would either walk or bike there. I was young and was not allowed to use the family bicycle yet, so I just walked there by myself. It only took me about half an hour from my house to the cathedral by walking. I usually stayed at the cathedral after Mass to play with other kids, especially on the weekends.

The cathedral was a beautiful structure built during the French colonial era with the European architecture of the medieval period. It was built inside a large church ground within almost a whole block near the city center. There were gardens inside the church ground with fruit trees and resident housing, and was fenced with high brick walls. It was a safe and fun play ground for kids to play inside the area. My parent had not been very happy seeing me playing at my home street because they didn't trust the boys in my neighborhood; however, they would allow me to play inside the church ground. Moreover, most of the people believed that the bombing jets would not target the church and it would be safe for us to play in there. It was a private place and all the priests and nuns knew each of us by name. The cathedral was built in one corner of the block. Next to the cathedral was a high bell-tower with a square base of strong rock walls. Standing on the flat top of the tower one could see the clear view of the down town area and the whole landscape of the city.

It was the culture of the church to ring the church bells once every hour during the daytime, slowly one time for each bell. But during the time there was Funeral Mass at the church, each bell was rung once and the whole sequence would be repeated after a short quiet moment. During those Mass times, I sometimes was asked to come all the way to the top of the bell-tower with two other boys. To control the exact ring sequence, each of us would sit on the structure beam by each bell to ring the bell directly with our hands until the Mass was over. Sitting up there by the bells, one could look through the ventilating spaces down to the church ground to observe the outside activities of the church. Inside the tower were three huge bells of different sizes hanged near the top area. There was a large metal wheel attached to each bell which was used as the pulley for the bell. The wheels were tied to the thick and long ropes with the tied end of the ropes lay inside the grooves at the edge of the wheels. The other loose ends of the ropes were dropped down to the second level of the tower. To ring the bell, the ringer would normally stand on the second level floor of the tower and pull the rope to turn the bell wheel and swing the bell. As the bell is swinging, the plunger hanging inside the middle of the bell would hit the bell wall and make the sound. However, during the Funeral Mass time, we had to hold the plungers by hand and hit the bells manually to control the exact sound sequence in a specific resonant period of the bells.

The bells sounded very loud and the whole town could hear them, but the sound was soft and would not hurt our ears even we were very close to them; although we would plug our ears while sitting up there for safety. I had heard that the bells had been made from some special alloy which was composed with gold and other precious metals so it could reverberate with high resonance but still warm and soft to human ears. The sound of the bells surrounded in the air making the atmosphere of the city seamed more peaceful during war time.

But it was more fun when ringing the bells before the regular Sunday Mass. At that time, we would ring the bells continuously with the ropes for a long moment. The bells were very heavy; after pulling the bell ropes down, we would sometimes hold tight to the ropes and, as the bells swung to the other side, they would pull us up on the air with the ropes and then back down to the floor. The bell ropes at that time worked as the swings in the park for the kids and we really enjoyed it.

There were rectory and convent, housing for the monks and the nuns living inside the church ground, located at two separated sides of the block. The space in the center was a large garden with open playing ground, walk ways, and a lot of big lichee, longan, and some other kinds of fruit trees. The church used the products from this garden for their additional income. Every year, the church would harvest many huge loads of the fruits from these trees to sell them to the retailers at the local market. In one side of the church ground next to the cathedral was the mulberry garden. The leaves from these mulberry plants were used to feed the silkworms which the nuns raised at their convent. Next to the mulberry garden was a huge concrete water container that used to collect and hold the rain water for the irrigation of the mulberry garden.

Near the center of the church ground was a large man-made mountain as high as a three-story building with an open cave at the base and was used as the place of Nativity. The man-made mountain had been built with large rocks long time ago. There were many small plants and moss grew naturally on it which made the mountain looked very genuine. In side the cave were the statues of Baby Jesus, Mother Mary, St. Joseph, the three Kings, the herds-men, and the animals.

Every year during the Christmas Holiday, the Nativity Place was decorated resplendently with colorful lighting and statues of many singing angels. There were a few hyacinth flower plants growing in front of the mountain area. At night the flowers in those plants emitted their fragrance around the area made it even more attractive. A few traditional religious music bands from the vicinities would come to the cathedral to perform their arts several days before Christmas Eve. Every Christmas Eve, the whole front yard inside the church ground would be full of people; many young people in the city, regardless of their religions, would come to the church ground to enjoy the spirit of the Holiday.

In contrast with the clean and well maintained front yard, behind the mountain was another garden with a lot of high trees with dense braches and leaves. The dense leaves covered the whole back garden area and made it much darker with very little sunlight. The ground was not well maintained and the dead leaves were thick on the ground which made the ground very muddy. There was also a large fish pond at the edge of the garden which the church used to raise tilapia fishes. Normally no one would want to go back there but I was always curious about this seeming freakish place; however, I was disgusted of walking without shoes on the muddy ground and never walk into this place; shoes were some luxurious items at the time.

One time while playing hide-and-seek in the front garden with other kids inside the church ground, I climbed to the back of the mountain from the front side to hide from other boys. While I was in the back side of the mountain, the idea of exploring the mountain and the back garden came to mind. I climbed all the way close to the top of the mountain and looked down the view of the back garden. While I was up there, I had a feeling as I was not in the church ground but some wild place. I observed many strange small plants and even some orchids growing at the high part on the back side of that man-made-structure.

There were usually a few altar boys staying at the church after Sunday Mass and we sometimes helped the priests with their daily house chores while playing around the area. There was a young priest living in the rectory who we called Father Thinh. He was still young and also had a tropical fish hobby. He raised a large pair of the angel fishes inside a glass tank in his room. The fishes had been matured and were almost the size of my palm.

His lovely pair of fishes spawned with a lot of tiny baby angel fishes swimming inside the glass tank around their parents as some clots of tiny dots; there must be at least three hundred of them. When I had a chance to come inside the priest room, I would stay by the tank to watch the fishes as long as I could.

The baby fishes were too small and needed to be fed daily by some special food. The priest now and then asked our kids to help him finding the food for his growing baby fishes. I often went out to get the mosquito larvae to feed my fish and knew some places which had stagnant rain water and a lot of tiny water creatures. The creatures were as small as the little dots and had a pinkish color. They lived in the stagnant rain water of the tropical climate during the summer time. With my spoon-net and a plastic bucket, I went to those places and got a lot of the tiny creatures back for him to feed his baby fishes. The little fishes were fed with live food and grew very fast. When the fishes were large enough, they were then transferred to two large ceramic jars in the back of his room. Later on the priest asked the old altar boys to sell most of the young fishes to the local pet store.

To appreciate for our help, the priest gave each of us several of the young fishes to take home; he gave me ten. I could not believe that I had so many of my favorite fishes that day without spending any money. I remember I had to walk a long way home while carrying the full and heavy water bucket with my fishes inside it. I could not walk straight home and had to make many stops on the road to rest, but I felt so happy that day. I didn't have the glass tank for my fishes then. It was expensive and kids would not have the money for it. I asked my mother for her large plastic bath tub. I filled the bath tub with aged water and put the fishes in there. My little angel fishes seemed to love their large home and grew healthily. The stripes on their bodies were getting darker each day. It was a joyful feeling to see the fishes growing healthy and swimming happily in side the clear water.

When winter came and the tank water needed to be warm, I moved my 'fish tank' under my plank bed in the middle of the house, the warmest spot, and hanged a light bulb close to the surface of the water. Adult people would have money to buy glass tank and the water heater, but I was happy with what I had then. The place I placed my fish tank was a little more difficult for me to change the water for the fishes; however, there was enough space under the plank bed to creep my head in there to feed and watch my lovely fishes. I still kept the beta fish but raising my new angel fishes became my most joyful activity at that time.

I obtained some white sand and put them at the bottom of my tank, and then got some water plants and planted them in there. My fish tank had become my little natural world and I spent most of my time at home around my new fish tank. Seeing my fishes grew healthly, I often dreamed about one day I would be able to breed a lot of my own baby fishes for my beloved hobby.

6. Running Away from Home

The bombing was still happened from time to time. People in the city had no choice but adjusted to the situation and went on with their normal daily life. When the bombing jets arrived to attack the city from above, most of the daily activities of the people on the ground were just suspended for a while during the assault but resumed right away after the jets left. One day I was playing at the street near our house with some other kids, suddenly, the city alarm siren went off; people were running to find some place to hide. The kids I was playing with ran to the shelters by the side of the Lap River. I usually just stayed inside our building during the air raid time, but that time I somehow followed and ran with the other kids and then got down into a zigzag trench.

After getting down there, more people were coming down and the tunnel was almost full. Some people were carrying a small bag of sugar and other even carrying a large bag of the dry provisions with them. I felt so stifled and uncomfortable and regretted that I had followed other people to this dirty place. I wanted to get out but the trench was packed and the aerial bombing was more frightened this time. While down there, the sound of the coming jets together with the explosions of the air defensive guns were tearing the air right above our heads. The roar from the jets was getting so close that it seamed like the attack were aiming right at our hiding location. Then I heard a terrible whistle of a fighting jet coming very close to us and right after that were a few deafening explosions. It was so close that the ground was shaking violently. Everyone panicked and got out of the tunnel and I followed them out too. Many other people also got out from the other nearby shelters looking confused and seemed frighten out of their wits. I heard someone shouted "run, run, there is unexploded bomb!" and a lot of people were running. I was caught off guard in the horrific situation so I ran with them too. As I was running, I saw one person was riding on the bicycle with an injured person in the back seat passing by us from behind. I looked at the person in the back seat and saw her clothes soaked with blood and all her body was covered with the red blood. The young girl had lost one arm and the blood was still coming out from the wound. That was the first time I was so terrified.

After running for a long distance, people started to scatter into different direction. I slowed down to breathe but kept on walking. I was thinking about getting back home but as I was looking back at the direction of my house, I still saw people coming out from that direction. Some more people were injured and their cloths were bloody too, so I kept on walking. I thought about my family and was worried for them but I was so nervous that my feet kept on walking. After running and walking for more than an hour and it was close to sunset time, I realized that I was walking alone by myself on a street far away from home. All the people who were running with me had scattered to different directions and I was very tired then.

I stopped and looked around the area. I recalled the street I stood was near the suburban area. I remembered one of my father's close friends was living close to that place. We had visited each other once in a while and all the members of the two families knew one another very well. The family lived inside a small village in the out skirt of the city not too far from the city main streets. I turned into a small dirt road and walked about twenty more minutes to get to their house. The door of their backyard was facing the small dirt road. I came and knocked on that door and the woman in the house opened the door, she was surprised to see me standing there. She asked me why I came all the way to their place just by myself. I told them what had happened to the area of our family and that our house might be bombed. At that time, there was no telephone to call so we could not know exactly what was going on with our house and had to wait for the new from the radio.

    The family let me stayed with them while waiting for farther information. Their house located at the rural zoning away from any heavy industrial factory and would not be the target for the bombing attack. The next day, from the radio, we knew that the bomb did not hit my homestreet but it was aimed at some factories near our house. I was at peace after hearing the good news. I wanted to go home then but the family members asked me to stay with them for a few more days to make sure it was safe before someone would give me a ride home with their bicycle.

    Staying there with the family was the first time I visited the rural area and I really loved it. There was a garden in every house around their neighborhood. The family had a large garden with many fruit-trees. The first time I was able to climb the guava-tree and to pluck its fruits with my own hands. The body of the guava-tree was so smooth that one can hold around the body of the tree and easily push the body up to large branch and lie on it. It was enjoyable lying on the guava-tree while eating its fruits up there. Even in a torrid summer days, it was cool and comfortable up there; especially the smell of the fresh guava leaves was very pleasant.

The air was much more comfortable around this village area than out on the streets. Walking on a large dirt road to at the back of the housing area was the wide open field of many huge square shallow lakes adjoined one another. The breeze over the lake water made the area much cooler than the city streets. The lakes were separated by the small dirt roads so that people could access each lake easily. People living in all the nearby villages grew a lot of lotus plants in these lakes. Most of families around this area made their living from selling their harvest of these flower plans.

The gorgeous lotus flowers rose above the immense fields of the wide green lotus leaves. The fresh air in the hint of the lotus flower scent created a halcyon atmosphere in the whole region which reminisced my peaceful days around the Tam Bac River near our home before the appearing of the bombing attack. In one lake, someone sitting inside a small basket boat was cutting the flowers and put them in her boat, perhaps for selling them that day. In the other lake, a couple other workers were wading inside the shallow lake to harvest the lotus roots.

I was curious and came close to the lakes. As I was at the edge of a lake, I looked down into the water and was fascinated to see so many mosquito larvae in the water at the edge of that lake. The larvae clotted into many large black lumps on the lake water surface. I was young and not thinking much about the bad and serious effect of the mosquito, I just thought about it as food for my fishes. Seeing so much mosquito larvae put me in mind of my beloved angel fishes and my family at home. I got back to the house and told our friend that I really missed my family and wanted to go home. The next day, one person of the family gave me a ride home.

7. My Father

My mother was delighted seeing me back home. Everyone in our family had been worried and was looking for me, but no body had thought that I had run that far away. From talking with my brothers, I knew that a few houses a block behind our place had been hit by a bomb. But the main target for the aerial attack had been the industrial area on the other side of the Tam Bac River. The pressure from the bomb explosions had blew away many wood planks on the surface of the suspension bridge and had put it out of order. My father factory had been sabotaged by the attack and he had stopped working at his job.

After the bridge had been damaged,

people either had to travel across the Tam Bac River by a small ferry-boat or they had to across the river by another steel bridge at another very far away location. But sometimes the ferry-boat was not available, especially early time in the morning, some young men who relied vaingloriously on their strength, would swim across the river from time to time when they needed to get to the other side of the river although that was an audacious behavior. I had witnessed several dead bodies of those who had been drowned at the river from swimming across it at the time no one was around the area to save them. Before the bombing, the river had taken only the lives of the pesky boys, but after the bridge was sabotaged, it had taken more lives of adult people too.

Since the day my father was no longer working, delivering his lunch was also removed from my daily activities. Instead, early every morning I had to boil some water and clean the tea-set for my father. Every morning after he woke up and right after he finished his morning hygiene, he would first come to the table and sat by the tea-set to prepare his tea. He would spend most of his time at that table to enjoy his strong tea habit. He made his tea very strong and used a tiny tea-cup for it. After his tea was ready, he would first smoke his special tobacco before the first tea-cup. The tobacco he smoked is called 'Thuoc Lao' (Lao

My Father

Tobacco). It is a particular tobacco of the Vietnamese and it is much stronger than regular cigarette. Probably, the special tobacco had been originated long time ago from some clan of the mountain people in Vietnam.

My father's tobacco pot was made by ceramic with meticulous decorative paintings. Inside the pot was half filled with water. On top of the pot was a small hole which was sealed with a small metal funnel to hold the tobacco. The bottom of the funnel was deepened into the water inside the pot. On the side of the pot was another hole which sealed with another smaller funnel above the internal fluid for the connection of the smoking pipe. A separated long pine would be used to such out the smoke from the pot. Although the pine was a very thin bamboo branch, it had been minutely decorated with some design pattern by some fire-marking technique. The pot had been designed so that the smoke would go through the water before getting to the lung of the smoker. Also the water inside the pot would make some pleasant sound while the smoke is sucking out from the pot.

To prepare for his smoking, he would roll some of the tobacco into a small ball with his thumb and a finger and put the ball of the tobacco into the funnel atop of the pot. After that he would take his long thin pine and would hold one side of it with his lips. The other side of the pipe was shaped to fit perfectly to the smaller funnel at the side of the pot and would be placed inside that funnel. There was always a small burning kerosene lamp and some spills set in a small can at a corner on the table. After he was ready, he would light a spill from the lamp and put the fire at the ball of tobacco in the top funnel. He then would take a few short breaths through the pine with his mouth to burn the tobacco. Every time he did that, I could hear the sound coming out from the pot. After a few short breaths, he would take a very deep long one to such all the smoke into his lung along with the hilarious sound. The ball of tobacco burned into a small red fire ball. He held his breath for a few seconds and blew the smoke out slowly. He took a cup of tea and then leaned back to the chair. His eyes were haft opened and he looked as he was high and in his bliss. He smoked now and then while reading at that table.

During the French colonial time, my parents had owned a grocery distributing business in North Vietnam and Lao Tobacco had been one of their trading products. From the stories that my mother often told us, my father was the one to ask about which type of Lao Tobacco was the best to use. He only needed to smoke the sample product and could tell the location where the tobacco had come from and what kind of environment it had been grown in.

    I used to be around my father and observed his tobacco smoking and was very curious about what it would taste like, but kids were not allowed to smoke. One time when I was home alone, I locked the house from the inside and tried to smoke his tobacco myself. I took a piece of the tobacco and rolled it into a very small ball. After putting the ball of tobacco into the top funnel, I did all the small steps in the smoking processes as my father usually did. When the ball of tobacco was all burned, I also took a deep smoke and held my breath. The coming smoke felt very smooth and comfortable at first, but when all the smoke was inside my lung, I felt so much pressure in my chess as my lung was going to explode. Right after that I tried to exert all my effort to blow out the smoke but it was too late, I could not control any part of my body at that time. My eyes were so blurry and the eyelids were so heavy. I closed my eyes and let the smoke slowly came out as much as possible by itself. I felt my heart was beating so fast. I lied down to bed and thought to myself that I was dying. After a long moment, I slowly felt better and better, and then back to normal again. I was so scared that day but had never told this incident to any one in my family.

My Adventure to The New World

Staying home without any work to do, my father just spent a lot of his day time at the tobacco pot and seemed not very happy, although he tried to hide it from us. I did not see him going out with his friend or inviting any of his friends to our home. He spent most of his time reading the religious books or the bible. Our family had a lot of books and many of those books were very old and has been conserved from the colonial time. By the time my father was still alive, those books had not been confiscated by the new government yet. I had not seen my father read much until he was out of work. In the afternoon was his church time. Everyday after lunch, he usually took a nap and when he woke up he would put on his dress, put a small folding paper-fan in the pocket at the back of his trousers, and went to the church. There was no mass in the afternoon by that time, but he just wanted to be there praying alone. I had been in the church a few times when there was no church activity inside; it was dark and very quiet. The space in side the church was so big that it echoed every walking step. I always felt a little chilled every time I was in there by myself. I imagined my father was kneeling by himself in that dark empty space and felt uneasy for him.

My father grew up during the French colonial era. When he was young man, he worked for a railway company and had many good

My Father

friends. After saving enough money, he married and with my mother, they started their own business. The business had been growing well and he had become an owner of a decent size grocery distributor. Too busy with the business, he had not joined the Vietnamese Revolution but had had a few friends as the early revolutionists at the time, and through his friends, he had donated a lot of his money to the revolution. However, after the victory of the Vietnamese against the French Colonial Administrator, the newly established government confiscated most of his property and dissolved his business. He had not been working for a long time, until the latter days of his life he somehow got a job as a security guard for the public factory near our home.

One time I was sitting alone with my father at home and I asked him if he was sad that his factory had been devastated and he could not work there anymore. He looked at me for a moment as he knew that I knew how he felt and said that he was sad because the factory had been ravaged but not because he was out of work. His salary had been too little anyway and he wanted to spend more time with his spiritual life. I wanted to ask him some more question but I did not know what to say at the time. I thought he was bored with his life but did not want me to know. Everyday at meal time, he often had a few small cups of the rice alcohol which was made locally by some private brewers and sold it in the black market. I always sat by him at our meal times. One time I asked him if I could try some of his drink. He poured some of his cloudy stuff into the little cup and gave it to me. I took a sip, it was so piquant but the smell was very pleasant. My mother chided him for letting me tried the alcohol but he just smiled and said "boy should try to learn and be ware of things."

At nighttime he sometimes secretly listened to a small radio in his bed. He set the radio close to his ear, and adjusted the volume of the radio just high enough for him to hear. I was curious and tried to come close to listen with him but he never allowed me to. Sometimes I saw him turning the knob on the side of the radio to search for his desirable channel and the volume of the radio was turning on louder by accident. At that time he would turn the volume down immediately as he was afraid someone might know what he was listening to. Later on I found out he was listening to the prohibited BBC Radio of the Great Britain, the Voice of American - VOA, and other radio channels of the foreign countries talking about situation of the Vietnam War then.

Another time I asked my father why our city was being bombarded; Is it because the American had wanted to occupy our country as I had heard from our public radio? My father did not answer me right away as he was thinking about if I was old enough to know about the subject. But later that day he explained to me that because North Vietnam was attacking South Vietnam and we were bombed because the American was an ally of South Vietnam. Until that time, I realized that Vietnam had been divided into two different regions of different governments.

After talking to my father that time, I started to pay more attention to the political situation of Vietnam. What I learned from our school children books was that South Vietnam had been occupied by the American and the American was trying to take over North Vietnam too. I realized the reason we were forbidden by our government to listen to those foreign radio channels were the difference in the contents they had broadcasted. My mother had once told us that our father was very patriotic when he was young. Although he did not like communism or involving in politics, he had donated lot of money to the revolution of the Vietnamese people against French Colonial Government.

I also wanted to know why our parents did not like communism. According to my father, the revolutionists had chosen communism only because communism could attract the poor people. Most of the Vietnamese people were in the poor working class at the time of the revolution and felt that they were being oppressed by a minority upper class and wanted to rebel. In order for the revolution to be succeeded, the early revolutionists need a lot of followers. By using the theory of communism as "working according to one's ability, enjoying as one's need" and the recently successful Russian Communist Revolution as an example, the early revolutionists had propagated and had attracted many people from the poor working classes into the movement. As the result from it, the forefront revolutionists had leaded the nation into the early success and had chosen communism as the new administration system.

    I did not understand much about politics and I had only heard the public radio often praising our government and our leaders. Many songs were often sang by both the children and adult choirs praising the revolutionists and our newly government on the radio everyday. I thought that my father had done some business with the French people during the colonial time and had the sympathy with the French, and perhaps that was the reason he did not like communism or our nation leaders. I once mentioned my opinion with him and he just smiled. After I insisted to find out what was in his mind, he educated me that for a nation to become richer, first of all, the leaders of that nation have to be both well educated and generous. The French had brought many good things to Vietnam, and under the French Colonial Government, there had been some high educated leaders, but they had only focused on the benefit of their own, not about the future of the Vietnamese. Vietnam had been getting poorer and poorer. When an elite group of Vietnamese people appealed to the French Colonial Government for some change, The French Colonial Government had not considered their request and that had leaded to the revolution. After the revolution, the main authority of the nation was in the hand of the working class people. However, the working class people usually had inferiority complex and envied toward the higher class and most of the high educated people in the country has been left unused. Therefore, the situation of the nation was not getting any better.

My father did not like communism and most the cadres in the government. To him the nation needed more magnanimous leaders who had broader vision, someone who cared not only about themselves and their relatives but more to the benefit of the whole community, and had good vision for the farther future of the nation. He always said to us "tien hoc le hau hoc van" (first learning about ethics and latter about skill). He believed our society was lacking ethical education and that the good leaders are the people who must know the root of the problem and should stress on the education of both ethics and skill at the same time.

I was not so interest in the educational subject but I loved to listen to my father. I thought he probably needed someone to talk to so I always tried to be patient and pretended that I understood what he said to me then. My father was more spiritual person than a political individual. There was time he had told me that the human body is the temporary residence of the spirits. According to him, there are good spirits and bad spirits living inside the human body and that is the reason why human could have both good and bad habits. He said we all need to pray daily for the good spirits to reside within ourselves. He had mentioned to me about many powerful leaders of the world who had often prayed before making any important decision. He strongly believed that people need to be both spiritual and intellectual to be balanced.

He loved to read about the stories of the Catholic Saints. One of his favorite saints was St Alexius. He admired the saint and had told us many times about the story of St Alexius.

St Alexius was born in Rome during

My Father

the fifth century in the reign of the Emperors Honorius and Arcadius. His parents, Euphemian, a Roman Senator, and Algas, were very wealthy. When St Alexius reached the age to marry, his parents chose a princess for him to marry. Immediately after the wedding celebrations, when normally the bride and groom would retire to the nuptial chamber, Alexius took flight from Rome and sailed to Syria. He then journeyed to Edessa in Syria, where he assumed the life of a beggar at the door of a church dedicated to Mary. He was also said to have served the sick in the hospital during his time in Edessa. Close to the end of his life, he went back to Rome where he met his father, Euphemian, who did not recognize him, an ill-clothed sickly beggar, but gave him employment allotting a corner under the stairs as his quarters. For seventeen years he thus lived unknown in his father's house, bearing the ill-treatment of the other servants in patience and silence. After years of hard work and inconspicuous humility, Alexius died in the under the stairs of his father's house.

The day the saint died was Friday, and my father had said that he could not live like the saint but when he dies he would like to die on Friday just as St. Alexius did.

8. The First Sea Travel

The first wave of bombard had stopped but my father was not going back to work anymore. One day, he said he wanted to visit his brothers and other relatives in his old hometown. After saying that, the next day he went to Hon Gai, a small beach town near Haiphong City, to visits many of our relatives and my oldest brother who was staying there with my cousin to learn some new trade from our relatives living out there.

After my father left home for a couple weeks, one afternoon, my mother called my other two brothers and me, together with my sisters to come and sit by her. When we all were sitting down around her, she said to us: "I just had a strange dream last night." And she looked very serious and worrisome. We all stayed quiet and listened carefully to her. She then went on: "In my dream, I saw the flesh on my arm was cut separately from the bone. I saw the white arm bone was exposed, but I did not see any blood coming out." After she said that, she looked down as she was deeply concerned about something was happening. Seeing my mother not happy, we all felt uneasy. After a short moment of silence, she looked up and said: "I think something is wrong with your father."

I was about to ask her why she thought so, but right at that moment, we heard someone knocked on our door. One of my brothers ran to open the door. A mail-man was standing behind the door with his mail bag on his side and a piece of paper in his hand. He handed my brother a telegram and left. My brother took the telegram back to my mother. The telegram had been sent by my oldest brother who was staying in Hon Gai at the time. The telegram read "Dad just died, mom and everyone come right away." As I heard my brother read aloud the telegram to my mother, I felt the inside of my mouth becoming bitter and the bitterness seemed getting stronger. I tried to swallow it down but I felt something strangled in my throat. I looked at my mom and saw her tear started to come out from one of her eyes. Everyone of us was petrified by the

The First Sea Travel

sudden bad new.

The next day, very early in the morning, my mother together with everyone else in our family went to the Binh Dock at the Binh River and bought ship-tickets to travel to Hon Gai. The easiest way to travel from Haiphong to Hon Gai that time was by waterway. After obtained our tickets, we all boarded the commercial ship docked not too far from the ticket boot. The ship was a decent size old one and there were about a hundred passengers boarding that day.

After all the passengers had boarded, the ship howled a long honk and started leaving the dock and slowly turned its head around. It moved slowly over the alluvial reddish river water away from the dock and passing the nearby city harbor. Once it passed the harbor, it slowly speeded up its speed and moved gradually faster. Looked through the window at our seat, the signs of some people still standing at the dock were getting smaller and smaller until they were just a few small black dots. The estuary was getting wider and wider as the ship coming out into the sea. After sitting with our mother for a while, we all went to the outside and stood at the front of the ship. As the ship was coming out of the estuary, the water was gradually getting clearer, and clearer, and then the ship was running over the sea blue water. It has come into the famous Ha Long Bay.

I had heard a lot about this fabulous bay and had seen its pictures somewhere before but that was the first time I literally traveled to the famous place; although we were in a grieved time, I felt a little excited. The islets started to appear out in front of us. It was just a few islets in the beginning and then so many limestone, schist islands appeared out on the surface of the turquoise water. Standing in the front section of the ship to contemplate, we felt the sadness of losing our beloved father was somewhat subsided. After a long moment of contemplating the surrounding we seemed forgetting from the time being and felt lost in legendary world of the wonderful nature. Looking ahead, the whole bay was a spectacular view such as the beautiful paintings of some talented artist that I had seen somewhere before. The islets had so many different shapes and sides. Either the ship was old that its motor was probably not powerful enough to propel the ship faster or it was not safe to move fast in this area, the ship just moved slowly over the surface of the bay water. It battled its way through the islands such as the ship captain wanted to show off the beautiful of the bay to the passengers that day. Travelling on the ship in the admirable landscape had literally taken our minds away from the sadness at that time.

My older sister knew more about the popular stories related to this area than any of us and she educated us about the legendary of the bay. There were a Man's Head Islet, which resembled a man standing and looking toward the mainland, a La Vong Islet resembled an old man fishing, and many other islets all over the place.

(La Vong was the name of a gift old statesman of the ancient time. Before he became a famous statesman; he had often stayed at a small bridge as an old fisherman holding a fishing rod without the hook, waiting for the king on his way passing by to have an opportunity to represent his political idea to the king)

As the ship went deeper into the bay, it passed by a couple of small islets standing right next to each other such as one small mountain was split into two separated halves leaning their summits toward to each other. They resembled the two roosters were fighting with each other and were called the Pair of Roosters.

When the ship passed by a big limestone island with a large cave showing it's opening on the surface of the water, my sister told us that it was the Dau Go (Driftwood) Grotto. She informed us that the name Driftwood Grotto came from the story of our resistance war against the Nguyen Mong invaders (Genghis Khan descendant's empire).

By the time the Mongolian Empire had taken the whole China and was trying to annex Vietnam in the south into their territory. In a decisive battle, General Tran Hung Dao was given an order to prepare many ironwood stakes to be planted on the riverbed of the Bach Dang River. When the river was at high tide, the wood stakes were hidden underneath the river water suface. At the time the war ships of the Mongolian Invaders came, they were lured deep into the narrow area close to land. When the tide was ebbing, the Vietnamese soldiers in their light boats then turned around and counter-attacked the invaders fiercely. The Mongolian Invaders were pushed back to the area with the embedded ironwood stakes, pounded into those stakes, and were all drowned. This battle had become one of the most epic victory of the Vietnamese against the Mongolian Empire. The Dau Go Grotto was used to store the stakes during the working process of preparing for this battle.

As the ship just passed the Driftwood Grotto into an open water area, I heard some one shout out "look! look!" from the middle section of the ship. We all turned and looked

The First Sea Travel

at the person and then toward her finger pointing out to the open water surface, a large rounded brown section, about a couple yards in diameter, of some mystic water creature jutting above the water surface. So many passengers came to one side of the ship to look at the mysterious animal. The ship was tilted heavily to that side and becoming very dangerous. As what would happen to me later on in my life, I somehow had had a picture of a boat a sinking into the water in the back my mind sometimes. Suddenly at that moment, that vision came to mind again and I was thinking about what would happen to all of us if the ship tilted over. Right at that moment, the ship captain came out and used a speaking-trumpet to warn everyone to get back to their seats. Fortunately everybody listened to his warning and went back to their places and the ship was balanced again. After the ship has been balanced, we went back out and stood at the door looking out for the strange animal, but it had disappeared and did not come back up again.

Getting close to the mainland, we passed by another island and there were a few small boats of the fishermen berthing around. When our ship was getting close to the island, I looked into the cave and saw a pole of limestone with a shape of a person standing inside near the opening of the cave looking toward mainland. My sister told us it was called the Trinh Nu (Virgin) Grotto. She also told us the legendary of this mysterious island.

Long time ago, there once was a young and beautiful fisherman's daughter, whose family was so poor that they were in service of the rich administrator of the fishing zone. The administrator liked the young girl so much that he forced the family to give him their daughter as a concubine. However, the young girl had already fallen in love with another young fisher man, and determined not to marry the administrator. The administrator got angry and exiled her to a wild island where she suffered from hunger and exhaustion. She was missing her boy friend and her family so much that she kept on singing everynight, until one night she turned into stone, still standing near the openning of the cave looking toward land. On that same night, her lover, knowing of her danger, rowed his boat in search of her. However, a tempest destroyed his boat, and he floated to a nearby island closer to mainland. In a flash of lightening, he saw her in the distant island, but his calls were driven away by the wind. In the final exhaustion, he also turned to stone. And that island was called Male Grotto.

It was said that until this day, on the full moon night, fisher men still often heard the voice of a young girl singing from inside the cave. I remembered when I heard to that part, I felt the goose bumps on my body even though we were in the middle of bright clear day. The singing sound had been probably created by the wind blowing through the stalagmites inside the cave, but some fisher men had asserted that it must be the voice of a young woman. I stood by the hand-rail out side the boat and imagined the suffering young couple was looking for each other in a stormy dark night out at sea, feeling the tormenting of the poor in those old days.

The sounds from the horn of the ship brought me back from my imagination. The ship was heading toward the dock of Hon Gai. Looking to the mainland was a very high limestone mountain standing along the coast, half on land and half in the sea. When the ship was getting close to the dock, the engine was turned all the way down and the ship moved slowly toward the dock. Looking upon the mountain was a poem carved on a flat stone cliff. The mountain was called Bai Tho (Poem) Mountain. In the fifteen century, Emperor Le Thanh Tong, who was also a poet, made an inspection tour of the North-East region. He stopped at the foot of the mountain, and inspired by the magnificent beauty of the surroundings, he wrote a poem. Later, he had the poem engraved on the wall of the mountain. The mountain was called Bai Tho Mountain since then.

The red tile roofs of a few houses slowly and gradually appeared in sight. The ship slowed down some more and finally stopped at the dock. All the passengers started getting out and onto the dock. Hon Gai Dock was right by the foot of Bai Tho Mountain. We did not have telephone by that time to inform our relative the time we arrived. So there was no one waiting for us at the dock. After everyone in my family got off the boat, we walked on the small asphalted road curving around the base of the mountain on our way to our relatives' home. There was no side walk on the left side of the road since the road was very narrow and right by the base of the Bai Tho Mountain. On the right side of the road were several little one-level resident houses with red tile roofs. After walking for about ten minutes, we passed by a small open market right by the right side of the road. Looking into the market, there were several people selling fresh sea foods at the out side area of the market. Hon Gai was a small peninsular and most of the people lived near the water were fishermen. They caught their fishes the night before and sell them at day time at this market.

After walking for another ten minute we came to the down town area with two-level and three-level houses on both sides of the streets.

The First Sea Travel

The streets in center of the town were wider with more traffics. I was a little tired and wondering how far we would have to walk before we get there, but then I heard the sound of the funeral music from distance. In our tradition, during the funeral, people hire a funeral musical band to play at the funeral site.

When we got to our relatives' house, many people were there inside the house with my father lying in a half opened coffin in the middle of room. He just looked as he was asleep inside the coffin. There were also several people of the funeral musical band sat nearby. The sound of the sad funeral music made the mourning site even more miserable. As soon as we got there, everyone was put on the mourning apparel, a white cloak made by simple material which was normally used for mosquito-nets. We all sat around the coffin together with my oldest brother and other relatives to mourn my father.

We were told that my father had been fine the days before he died. My brother was sitting with him in my cousin's house that day and my father said that he was feeling not well. After saying that, he went up stairs to the second floor and my brother went up with him. My father lied down to bed and told my brother to leave him alone to rest. My brother left him and went down. After a while he went back up to check on my father. When he got up there, he found my father was already passed away in that bed. My father probably suffered from a sudden heart attack and died abruptly. It seemed that my father had known ahead the day he would pass away. He died on Friday afternoon exactly as he had once said he would. He was only fifty six years old when he passed away.

As our mourning tradition, my father was left lying in the coffin for three days. After the mourning period, his coffin was carried on foot by men to the cemetery to be buried. The cemetery was on a hillside far from our cousin's house. The funeral music bands and all family members and friends followed the coffin as a long line of people moving though town. The music was played along the line of mourning people walking on the streets. When we got to the burry site, my father was buried next to my deceased uncle's tomb at the Catholic Cemetery on that hill at the out skirt of the town.

A few days after my father was buried, we went back to the Hon Gai Dock to get the ship tickets to go back home. That day, the line of people waiting at the ticket boot was very long. As I stood waiting at the dock with my family, I looked upon the Bai Tho Mountain and saw many little yellow monkeys playing on the trees at the middle area of the mountain. It was the first time I saw so many monkeys in their natural habitats. I kept looking up there until I heard my mother calling me; it was boarding time. We all got on the ship to travel home.

When we were on the ship, I asked my mother about the monkeys on the mountain. I wondered if those were wild monkeys or someone was raising them. My mother was ridiculed by my question. She said with a smile: "Of course they are wild monkeys." I asked her why no one had caught them and she told me that there was a family living at the base of the mountain and the monkeys often came down to play at their houses when no one was home, and sometimes devastated their homes. The monkeys liked to imitate human and had done different human-like activities. One day that family made glutinous alcoholic rice and ate the alcoholic rice at the out side of their house and let the monkeys saw them eating from the distance. They left the left over alcoholic rice in the out side and left the house. They got back to the house after a while and saw several drunken monkeys lying near the rice. They caught all of those drunken monkeys. But the monkeys were smart, they learned to avoid people and only live at some perilous areas of the mountain after that.

I was fascinated by her story and wished that someday I would be able to go exploring the area and visiting the people living up there.

9. My Mother

After everyone had come home, my mother then told us about the meaning of her dream the day before we went to Hon Gai for the funeral of my father. To her, the dream had foreshadowed the decease of my father. She said that her relationship with my father had been like the bone and the flesh of the same body, but there was no blood relation. In her dream, when she saw the flesh on her arm was separated from her bone without seeing any blood, she knew that something wrong had happened to my father, and it turned out to be the day my father was passing away.

Without the aerial assault, life in the city was back in normal again. My oldest brother also moved back home to live with the family a few days after the funeral of my father. He would then be the head of the house hold according to our culture. My first sister married, moved out, and lived with her husband's family. My second brother was over eighteen and was at the military duty age, he was mandated to join the North Vietnam Arm Force as most of the other young men at the time. My third brother and my other sister had dropped out of school since the time the school closing in the city area during the first wave of aerial bombard. They both stayed at home to help my mother with our family financial affair. I was the only one in our family attending grade school at that time.

My brothers were trying to look for a job with any public factories, but it was very hard to find any job those days. With our family's history, it was nearly impossible for them to obtain a decent government job. Before the Revolution, my parents were merchants; with the new government policy, they were listed as former capitalist people. More than that we were catholic family; therefore, no government organization would hire us.

Fortunately, my first brother was a self-taught person and had learned some trade skills. After coming back home, he obtained books to develop and master his new galvanizing skill. At the time, most of the high level technical books were in French language. Fortunately, he knew French and somehow obtained those technical books to perfect his trade. With the help of some good friends, he obtained a permit from government agency to work at home as cooperation unit and also a contract with a local government manufacture to galvanize zinc for it new product.

The pre-galvanized screws were packed inside the carton boxes and brought to our home. My brothers set up all the necessary equipments right at our backyard. It required only a small area and some simple equipments for the work, mainly included a concrete tank of acidic fluid and some large plastic buckets. My first brother was responsible for the technical aspects and the paper work for the business. The second brother was in the army, so my third brother was responsible for the physical work of the production.

My brothers made several special metal frames with a lot of tiny hooks to hang the screws into. The screws, one by one, would be placed into the hooks on each frame. The frame full of new screws would then be hung at one of the poles on the brim of the chemical tank and the screws were deepened in the acidic fluid inside the tank. A large zinc plate was hung at the other pole on the tank and was also deepened inside the fluid. The two poles were connected to an electrical device which produced electrical direct current through the two poles. After a certain amount of time, the screws inside the tank would be plated with zinc. The frame of finished screws would then be taken out of the tank and the finished screws would be shaken into a large plastic bucket of fresh water. After the screws were washed cleaned of the chemical and dried, the dried screws would then be packed into the carton boxes and shipped back to the manufacture.

My mother also worked at home. She brought back home the blank pillow covers from a local cooperative producers and hand-embroiled the decorative flower on the pillow covers for them. My sister, the younger one, was helping my mother in some of her broidering and house works. Most of the house hold chores were done by my sister by that time.

I was attending grade school. My school was about half an hour walking distance from home. School started at eight in the morning, and it would be over at noon. The second grade class was my first class in public school since I had been home school previously. My first teacher happened to be the lady living at the third level of our duplex. I usually walked back with her after school and sometimes helped

My Mother

carrying her school stuff on our way home. At the end of that school year, she prepared the award certificates for all her outstanding students and there was an extra blank left over. To appreciate for my help, she wrote my name on the extra certificate and gave it to me.

I brought that certificate home and showed it to my mother. I could not forget the smile my mother had that day. She was so delightful! She put the certificate into a very nice frame and hanged it on the wall right in the center of our house. Perhaps she tried to motivate me to do well in school. My mother had never asked me to do anything if I was sitting at the studying desk with my school papers in front of me. I took advantage of that and sometimes just sat at my studying desk to read some of my favorite old friction stories.

Next to the studying desk were a lot of old books that our family had had since the colonial time, some legend stories, some Chinese old legend history books, and many books in French language that I had no idea what they were. Later on the Service of Culture & Information Office found out that we still had these old books. They sent their police to our home and confiscated all our books, even the technical ones. My brother entreated the police not to take away his technical books, but the police said that those books were in French and they could not know for sure the content of them. They just took them away and told him to appeal to the Service of Culture & Information Office. We lost all our precious books since then.

Everyone in my family was busy with our family works during the day time; however, at night after diner, my brothers and sister often went out with their friends. My mother rarely left the house except to go to church. She liked to read the bible in her spare time. My sister had tried a few times to invite my mother out to watch a movie at the theater close to our house, but my mother had always refused her invitations.

I sometimes liked to hang around the neighborhood with other kids my age but was not allowed to get to far from home. I was the youngest and my mother wanted me to be around the house when all my brothers and sister were not home so I would be able to hear her call when she needed any help. Going out and playing with the neighbor kids was very tempting, but one night my mother asked me to sit by her and she read the Bible stories for me. That was the first time I listened intently to the Bible and the stories literally brought me back to the ancient times when God was physically living with human on Earth. Those stories were interesting and really intrigued me.

My Mother

That day, she was reading the story of Jesus Christ praying alone in the Gethsemane Garden the very day before his crucifixion. I was sitting next to my mother and I looked into her book and saw a picture of Jesus kneeling by a large rock in a gloomy garden as he was looking upon the Heaven and was praying. Listening to the story while looking at the painting, I felt very sad! Perhaps at our young age, we were easily agitated. When she read to the part that Jesus was troubled and deeply distressed that he sweated with blood. I was moved into tear. My mother paused and turned to me as she saw tear was coming out of my eyes. She asked me:

"You are crying because you have to stay home alone with me tonight?"

I just shook my head. It was the first time I learned that a human being could sweat out with blood. The individual must be in extremely sorrow at the moment. I said to my mother:

'I just felt for the pain of Jesus.'

She put down her bible and held me in her arms. I took a few deep breaths to fight back my tear and then asked my mother:

'Mom, according to the bible, Jesus is the son of God and has all the divine power, why he let himself went through so much pain?'

"Because God loved people so much that he let his only son went through all the painful experiences and was finally crucified on the Cross to redeem our sins." My mother slowly and clearly explained to me:

I thought about what my mother just said but did not understand then, I told her:
'I don't understand. Mom, can you explain for me?'
My mother turned and looked deep into my eyes, with her hands placed on my shoulders she said softly:
"For a person's soul to go to heaven after this life on earth, the person has to be free from any sin. However, human being had chosen a sinful path and just getting deeper and deeper into it. To save our souls, God's only son became flesh and dwelt among us; he lived a human life just like us but without sin. He went though all the humiliated and painful experiences and finally was nailed on the cross and died so that who believe in His Name and truly appreciate his work would be saved and would have the right to become the children of God."

I thought about what my mother said. However, something was still not clear in my mind, so I asked her again:
'God created all human. Why have God not made us all perfect and without any sin?'
After a moment of silent, my mother said:

"To be perfect is to be wise enough and having the strong will to refuse bad things, and God loved us so much that God let us to have the freewill to choose for ourselves. Don't you remember that we human were all created by God from dirt?"

That night in bed, I thought about what my mother said that day, but the more I thought about it, the more I got confused. I was tired and fell asleep. The daily activities kept my mind off the topic of our conversation that day. Until one day I came to one of our neighbor's house, I saw a statue of Buddha and it got me curious again. I noticed that most of our neighbor families were either atheists who only worshiped their ancestors or Buddhism who worshiped Buddha. I talked to some of our Buddhism neighbors and they said that Buddhism was our nation religion and Catholic was introduced to Vietnam from the foreigners. I went home and asked my mother:

'Mom, is Buddhism our nation religion, and Catholic is religion of the foreigners?'

My mother was ridiculed by my question, she smiled:

"There is no border line in religion. By the way, Buddhism did not start in Vietnam either; it had been introduced to Vietnam before Catholic. Catholic was the teaching of the disciples of Jesus Christ, and it started in the Middle East. It was introduced to Vietnam by the very brave and dedicated European missionaries, and it still exists in our country today is because of all the sacrificing that our ancestors had gone though."

I started to think more about religious topic and wanted to ask my mother about Buddhism.

Although I knew that most of the old Vietnamese women had not been fortunate to have formal education. In our old tradition, the girls had neither been allowed to or their family had not had any chance for them to attend school in the old days. My mother had been in the same situation, she only knew how to read and write. I had been told that my grand father was a herbalist, but during his life time, the French soldiers often came to perform the mopping-up operation in their area and people in his village had to evacuate away from their village often; therefore, it had been very hard for him to do his herbal collection business. At that time my mother was a teenager and she had to travel from village to village in helping my grand mother with her long distance trading business. She married my father when they both were very young. Both my parents had not known each other before they married; the wedding had been arranged by their parents. After their wedding, my mother moved in to live with my father's family but they were not even sleeping in the same bed for a long time.

My Mother

A few years after their marriage, they moved out and started their own family. My mother had worked very hard and had been always busy, but she loved to read especially about religious genre, and she had read those books everynight before her bedtime.

Another day I asked my mother about Buddhism, she explained to me that Buddhism is the teaching of Siddhartha Buddha and Buddha was just a person like us. His name was Siddhartha, and was a prince of the noble Gautama family. He was born in northern India about five hundreds year before Jesus Christ. His father hoped their son would become "a universal monarch," the emperor of all India. At nineteen, he married a neighboring princess, and had one child. He was living in luxury, but became more and more unhappy inwardly. He decided to leave home and wandering in the forest to seek the true meaning of life. After many years of hard life and meditation, he was enlightened under the Bodhi-tree and became Buddha (the enlighten one).

I was again intrigued and wanted to know more about Buddha. Later on I sometimes asked our Buddhism neighbor but most of them did not know much about Buddha's teaching. Another time I asked my mother again about what was Buddha's teaching and why people worshiped him?

"He taught people to practice Buddhism to eliminate life suffering". My mother said.

I said to her:

'I know many families whose religion is Buddhism and that was what they told me too, but their lives are not much different from other people's.'

My mother explained:

"According to Buddhism, there are many cycles of life, and all living things would be reborn again and again into different life forms. This life on earth is full of suffering. People practiced Buddhism to become enlightened and would be able to control their soul and would be born in Paradise in the next life, where there is only happiness. However, it is very hard for us to become enlightened. Since the time Siddhartha Buddha still living on earth, there have not been many individuals be enlightened. Especially in our life time, there is almost no one be enlightened. Siddhartha Buddha knew ahead and had mentioned about this in his teaching. However, Siddhartha Buddha also taught that Amitabha Buddha, the highest one, would come down for the salvation of the human souls. That is why many Buddhism people practiced chanting the name of Amitabha Buddha. The whole emphasis is on faith, and faith is believed to be sufficient for the salvation."

My mother paused and looked at me as

she waited for me to rewind in my mind and absorbed what she just said, then she continued:

"And I believe that Amitabha Buddha is the Lord Jesus Christ who had come for the salvation of our souls so that who ever believe in His Name would be saved. The Name just sounds different in different languages and cultures."

I thought about what she said for a moment and it started to make sense to me. I asked her again:

'So as long as I believe in Jesus Christ, I can still do bad thing and my soul will be saved anyway?'

"If you strongly believe that Jesus Christ had loved you so much that he had died just for your sins, you would not do bad thing intentionally and sin again, would you?" She asked.

After a long moment of deep thought, I asked again:

'What happen to the people who do not believe in Jesus?'

"That would depend on their thoughts and actions during their lifetime. The more good deed they do, the better. Their souls may be reborn into some life form of this world and restart their learning process with a new life, or staying in sorrow at a different dimensions that we don't know about." She said.

I realized that I would never comprehend everything she said. But I still asked her another question:

'Mom, I talked with one of our old atheist neighbor and he said that we just need to live kindly and do not do bad thing to other people and that should be good enough. We do not have to follow any religion. Religions just divide and create conflict among people. Is that true?'

My mom did not answer me right away. She put one arm around me and looked to a far distance. After a while, she said:

"It is good and very important to live kindly and not to do bad thing to others. However, it is still not enough since we are human being with many weaknesses and can never become perfected. We need help from God and that was why God had sent his only son, Jesus Christ, to save us. We all should appreciate his love and have faith in him. We also have to live wisely since there are many bad people in this world who exploit religions to gain the benefit for themselves, and that divided people, not religions."

As she said the last sentence, my sisters walked in. My mother prepared some chores for my sisters to do. I went and sat by my special fish tank with many different thoughts in my mind. My angles fishes became my quiet friends every time I was in distress or confused. Watching the fishes swam so peaceful in the tank brought me calmness. I wanted to ask my mother some more questions, but she was busy with my sister that day.

I intended that I would someday spend more time on this topic with my mother, but by that time, I also participated into some church activities with other catholic kids on the weekends, and spent most of my weekends in the cathedral. I also just had a new friend from my class and we both liked to do our home works together at night in my house. All the busy daily activities steered me away from the subject.

10. The Second Wave of Bombard

The galvanizing business had helped our family during the tough economic period. But after a couple years of peacetime, the aerial attack was returning again. This was the second wave of American bombard. This time the attacks were happening more frequent and more disastrous; the alarm siren went off everyday, sometimes two or three times in twenty four hours.

One night the air raid siren suddenly went off in the middle of the night. We were asleep and felt a little hesitant to get out of bed but the loud explosions wakened up everybody in our family. We all ran down and got into the space under the concrete stairs. The hiding place was already packed by the time we got down there. There were not enough places for everybody in the building; therefore, only kids and women were given priority to stay in there, many others just stood nearby. I was given a spot inside next to my mother. Since the start of the second wave of bombing, more people were using this hiding place. The area around the stair base was crowd with many sleepy people that night.

    This time the attack was frightfully violent. The terrible sound of the coming jets seemed so close to our area. The ground artilleries and the air defensive missiles fired onto the air continuously. The quiet and peaceful night has turned into a night of consternation. After it happened for about ten minutes, the sounds of the fight jets were getting farther. The ground guns also slowed down along with the heart beats of all the people in the area. A few people were standing up to go back to bed, but right at that moment the fight jets were coming back again. This time, the jet sounded much deeper and farther as of new and different kind of bombarder. I heard someone standing in the outside area said: "B52, that is the sound of the B52 bombarder." I had no idea what B52 was, but everyone seemed so nervous when they heard the sound. Following the scary sound were the continuous explosions of several bombs, one right after other; it were so close that we could feel the violent change in the air pressure, and the building vibration lasting longer this time. The praying sound of the women inside the hiding place was getting louder each time they heard the sound of a bomb explosion.

After the sucessive explosions of the bombs, it was quiet again. This time, the bombarders had really left the city. People were going back to their rooms but no one could go back to sleep. Many people looked worrisome, standing around talking with one another about how scary and closer the explosions had happened this time. We sensed something new and scarier would follow the bombard soon.

Early the next morning, the local government official came to each house in our neighborhood and announced that we all need to evacuate from the area. The location of our area was too close to the industrial zone and it had become the target for the B52 planes which were on the program to carpet the whole area with bombs.

Every family in our neighborhood prepared quickly for the evacuation. My family packed up each person's personal stuffs and temporarily moved out to live with a friend not too far from our home. It was only less than half an hour walking distance but it was far enough from the evacuation zone. We had to

My Adventure to The New World

stop our family business due to the evacuation. My brothers were disappointed and very sad but we had no other choice. All schools in the city were closed again.

There was not enough room in our friend's house for all of us; therefore, my oldest brother moved out and lived with his friend at a different place. The family arranged a corner of the house as a living quarter for my mother, my sister, and me. My third brother slept with the son of the family. Our friend's family only had one son at the age of my brother and they were best friends; therefore, my brother seamed to enjoy staying there with them. But I had no friend there and it was boring for me living there. I missed my angel fishes so much. I worried that my fishes would be starved since no one was home to feed them.

Right after we moved out, there were several additional bombards at the area near our house and then it was quiet down again.

When the air rage was quiet down, I decided to go back home to feed my fishes. One afternoon, I obtained some live blood worms in a plastic bag from a tropical fish store near our friend's house and sneaked to my mom's bed to get the key for our house while she was napping. With the key and some blood worms, I walked back home by myself. When

I came close to the area of our neighborhood, the street leading to my house was blocked by a long wood bar with a large warning sign hanging in the middle of it. There was a row of big letters "Stop! There is unexploded bomb in this area" on the sign. The area was so quiet and there was no sight of anyone on the streets. I stopped at the warning sign thinking that I only needed to sneak in and out very quickly, but my heart was beating heavily. Not only because the unexploded bomb may go off anytime, I was also afraid that some local government official might see me sneaking into this forbidden area. After looking around to make sure no one around, I sneaked my body through and under the blocking bar and ran fast into the area. When passing a ruined building block, I recalled the time before the evacuation, this block had been the living quarters of many families. But this time it had changed to a ruin deserted place; a bomb had dropped by a building near the street and only part of the building was left standing. I was so nervous but kept on running toward my house.

Once I got to my town-house, I ran up stairs, opened the door, and immediately got to my fish tank under the plank bed. I was so happy to see all my fishes were still healthy. The fishes were scared away when I bended my head close to the tank. But then they all come back up as the clot of blood worms was dropped down. I watched as they disputed the worms until they were all full and slowing down on feeding. The rest of the worms sunk at the bottom. I was competing with time and filled the tank with some additional water in the water container at the backyard. I looked down at the fishes one last time before running back out of the house. I locked our home behind me and then ran away out of the dangerous zone.

We could not stay at our friend's house too long since the space in their house was limited. Although the family was nice and treated us kindly, my mother contacted the cathedral and asked for their permission to move in and stay in the church ground for a while. The church accepted our request. So we packed up again and moved to live inside the church ground.

There were two other families had moved in and lived in the there before us. Inside the church ground, there was a large community center which was normally used as a dining hall for the priests and the monks. We all were allowed to sleep at night on the floor of that dinning hall. The floor of the dinning hall was tiled and clean. We just set our sedge mats on the floor and would rest in there. At night, we could hang the mosquito net over the sedge mat to prevent us from mosquito bite.

Next to the dining hall was the main kitchen. The helpers and some nuns would prepare meals for the priests there. We were allowed to cook our meals in there too. But we all would clean up our stuffs, set them into a small area by the side of the hall, and would leave the hall before the meal times. A thick plate of iron was hung at a tree near the front door of the dining hall. Two times a day, one at noon and one around 5:30 PM, an old servant would come out there and would strike the metal plate with an iron club three times. After hearing the sound of the gong, the priests and the monks would come down to dine.

When the priests came to the dining hall, their meals were usually set readily on the tables; there were two long tables and a shorter one at the middle, which were placed together as the letter U. The bishop always sat in the center of the middle table with the other priests. A huge painting of St. Peter holding the Key of Heaven in one of his hands was painted on the wall behind the sitting place of the bishop. All other monks sat around at the two other tables. The nuns had their own place and were not eating at this place with the monks and the priests. Meal would start after the blessing prayer and usually last for half an hour. After their meals, the helping staffs would come and cleaned up the dining tables. After that we all could get back to the dining hall again.

Since the evacuation time, my mother had no longer worked with her embroidering business so she would do most of the daily chores without my help. I was allowed to play freely within the inside boundary of the church ground. I and other kids loved to climb the tall longan trees in the garden and searching for the bird nest up there. Playing hide-and-seek was fun in there too; there were so many places to hide. When we heard the alarm siren, we all would get inside the bell tower. The base of the tower was built very thick with large rocks mixed with concrete. We all believed that even a bomb drops nearby, the base of the tower should sustain its structure and we would be safe in there. In addition to that, we believed the bombarders would never target the church anyway.

Next to the bell tower was a huge man-make-mountain. The mountain together with the bell tower separated the whole area into two halves. The landscape in the front garden was well maintained with some flower plants and the decorative stable of nativity at the base of the mountain. Behind the tower and the man-made-mountain were the garden with many fruit-trees, vegetables, and a large square fish pond with a lot of tilapia fishes in there. The boundary of the pond was built with concrete walls about chest high except the opening with the stairs down to the water. The water inside the pond normally filled up to the last few steps down the pond.

The convent was in a long housing area close to and facing the pond. The nuns would cook and eat in their own places in that housing area. After their meal, they would often wash their dishes in the pond.

One time I came to the pond while a nun was cleaning her dishes. The working nun got down the pond and stayed at the first submerged step in the water to wash their dishes. As she washed out the left over food from her dishes, a lot of little baby tilapia fishes came up very close to the nun to feed on the left over food in the water. It was joyful to see so many little fishes coming so close to human without fear. But seeing the little tilapia fishes competing for food at the side of the nun, my angel fishes at home came to my mind again. So I decided to go home to feed my fishes again.

Like the last time, I took the key from my mother's baggage and went to another tropical fish store near the church. I bought some blood worms from the fish store and went back home. When I was one block away from my house, the whole area around the block had become more deserted and dreary this time, more buildings had been either ruined or totally destroyed. The wood bar blocking the incoming area that I saw the last time perhaps had been blew away. I ran pass several collapsed buildings and saw a huge bomb crater in the ground near the street with some rain water inside. I had a strange feeling of sadness, afraid, and a little angry. But right at that moment, I was startled by the air-raid siren and was very scared. I ran to a collapsed brick building and hid at a left over corner of the building. I was thinking: if something bad happen by this time, there is no one around to help. But then I realized that the jets would not attack at this place again. They would not squander their bomb to the already destroyed area twice. That thought calmed me down a little but I was still afraid that there might be some unexploded bomb in the area which could explode anytime. With both my hands covering my head tightly, I still heard the sound of the fight jets was getting louder as they were coming closer. But just as what I thought, the jets flew pass the place and targeted at some other area far from where I sat. After a few minutes, all the bombarders left the city again.

When the city sky was quiet again, I stood up and walked fast to my house. When I got to the building of our apartment, I saw the door and all the windows were wide open. In the first floor of the town house, broken glasses, debris, and broken pieces of furniture were all over the ground floor. I ran onto the stairs, got to the second floor and looked inside our living area; my thick and strong plank bed had been totally destroyed. Some small pieces of wood were scattered on the floor and my fish tank had vanished. I got closer and saw a large open hole on the floor with the size of a dining table. Looking through the hole down to the first floor level was a huge slab of stone lying deep in the ground. Looking up to the ceiling, there were a hole at the ceiling and one at the roof top of the building. A huge slab of stone, by the size of four feet long, two feet wide, and one and half feet thick, which had been buried deep in the ground as part of the curb for the side walk of some nearby street had been flung up high on the air by the explosion of a bomb and had dropped at the roof of our town house. It had gone through the roof of the building, through one bed on the third floor, through the third floor, through my plank bed, through the second floor of our living room, through one more bed at the first floor, and then deep into the ground. The stone lay in a shallow hole in the ground of the first floor. The second and third floors of the building were support by very strong wood beams. However, the stone was not broken and stayed in its original shape in the ground. It was incredible! I could not believe my eyes. My fish tank probably had gone down with the stone through the hole to the first floor and had been broken apart; all my lovely fishes were gone! I had spent so much effort to raise the school of fishes with hope that one day I would be able to select a few good pairs to breed; now everything was gone. I was stunned for a moment and then my eyes were profusely overflowing with tears. After a moment distress, I wiped off my tears and went back to the church.

When I got back to the church ground, I did not tell my mother about my trip for I knew she would scold me and would keep me in her sight all the time. After knowing what had happened to our home and my fishes, I was depressed and often feeling down, became quieter, and didn't want to play any games with other kids in the area. During the depression time, I started to hang out with a new boy named Bien, a boy one year older than me and was not a talkative altar boy. His family was not living in the church ground and he was not playing around other kids in the area. Bien was the only one I felt I could share my feeling without getting into trouble with my mother.

Bien came from a poor working family. He had four brothers and all of them were teenagers, he had no sister. His home was located at an area near the out skirt of town far from the church. There were also a few light factories near his house; however, it was not a major industrial area and hence was not in the bombing target zone. His mother was a proprietor of a small tea-shop at their house. It was called tea-shop but it simply included a low table and some small stools set near the side walk in front of their house. She prepared tea in a big tea pot and insulated the pot to keep it warm. Her customers were mainly the construction and factory workers who worked at the factories nearby. They normally came to her shop for a cup of tea during their break times. While having tea, they usually bought some cookies or a couple of cigarettes and would smoke while sitting at the table in front of his home.

Bien often helped watching the shop for his mother while she was busy with other chores. A time while sitting alone watching the shop for her, Bien took a cigarette from the used cigarette box at the shop. He brought that cigarette with him to church; he had probably stolen some cigarette from his mother and had smoked before. That day after mass, when everyone has left, Bien invited me to the corner behind the bell tower. It was in the afternoon and no one was around. When we both sat down side by side at a hidden place, Bien took

out the cigarette, showed it to me, and said:
"Do you ever smoke before?"

I was a little surprised, I said to him:

'No, my mom will whip me if seeing me doing that."

He lighted the cigarette and smoked a few puffs. He then handed me the burning cigarette and asked me:

"You want to try?"

'No, I should not' I said.

Bien took another puff and handed me the cigarette again:

"Hey, just one puff"

'No, thanks' I insisted.

Bien was upset; he stood up, and walked away.

I sat there until he was out of sight hoping that he would come back, but he did not. I sadly went back to the dining hall and stayed there with my mom. The next few days, Bien did not want to hang out with me anymore. I felt sad and decided to approach Bien. I waited for him near the door of the church dressing room where he would come out after Mass. When I saw him walked out, I ran to him and said:

'Hey Bien, do you bring your cigarette with you? I want to try it.'

"You will?"

Bien tried to hide his smile of satisfaction from me. We went to a hiding area and he lighted up another cigarette he had with him. Just as the last time, he took a few puffs and gave the cigarette to me. Remembering my bad experience with my father's tobacco, I took a soft buff, blew out the smoke, and handed the cigarette back to him. Bien did not take it back; he looked at me as I was cheating and said softly:

"You are not truthful! you did not swallow the smoke down."

I took another puff and swallowed it down; immediately I felt terrible and coughed and coughed heavily for a while. Bien smiled with complacence. But from that day, he never make me smoking with him anymore. we hung out with each other again and became close friends since. Except for the bad smoking habit, Bien was a nice and more thoughtful person than most of the boys at our ages. When I was with him, I could share many of my thoughts with him and felt very comfortable.

After staying in the cathedral for a couple of months, the city official came and ordered all the families who were living inside the church ground to move out to the countryside. It was illegal that the church had allowed us to live in there without permission of the city. We had no choice but followed their order. At that time, under the communist government, people had to report to the local government office if they had guess came and stayed in their home more than three days. The church had not reported our staying to the city authority. After helping us for a few months, the city finally found out about our stay and ordered the church to comply with the city.

11. Life in the Countryside

It was the summer of the year 1972 and was a very hot summer. The Vietnamese called it 'The Red Fire Summer' because of the violent aerial firing from the air-defense-artilleries almost everynight in the major cities and the fierce ground fighting near the Demilitarized Zone, but it was also true for the torrid summer we had that year. One day early in the morning, my brothers and one of my sisters gathered at the Dinning Hall in the cathedral to pack up our stuff and to help my mother moving to the countryside. We left the church ground in a hurry and without a chance for me to say good-bye to Bien, my deer childhood friend.

From her friends, my mother got an offer from a farmer family in Thuy Nguyen, a village in the suburban vicinity of the city, for my mother and me to stay and live with them.

It was a long ride under the burning sun to the countryside. My mother and I were sitting on a tricycle my mother hired from an old man in the city. The man was about fifty years old but his body still looked firm and he was an agile and active person. He rode the tricycle and my two brothers and my sister biked along the way. It took us more than three hours before we arrived to the remote village. Fortunately, there was no major aerial assault that day. Once we got to the edge of the village, there was only a small dirt road to the family and was it was hard for the tricycle to travel on it; hence, my mother paid the tricycle owner for the ride and we all walked on that road for another half hour to the family.

The family was not just any typical peasant family; they seemed to have a decent quality property compared to most other farmer families living in the area. The owner of the family was kind and very hospitable to us. They prepared to meet us on the day we came and had prepared a room for us to rest as they knew that we would be tired when we arrived. The room they reserved for us was just a small room with one bed in it. After sitting at their house for a while for our courteous greeting conversation, my brothers and sister had to bike back to the city to live with our other family friends. There was only enough room here for my mother and me. The people of the family looked strange to me as I had never met them before. I didn't know how my mother had obtained the connection with the family, but I did not ask for more information since I was so excited of being able to live in the countryside for the first time.

The family had four members: the couple was in their fiftieth with a teenage daughter and a boy about my age. They had another older son but their older son had jointed the army and had died a year ago. The picture of the deceased young man in army uniform was placed high at the altar in the middle of the main living room with some burning incenses in front. Their old wooden house was residing on a large lot of farm land. The house had only two rooms adjoining each other. The members of the family lived in the larger main living room. The smaller room which they used for storing harvested rice was prepared for us to stay in there; the unused space could fit only a small bed and had been used at times by one member of the family. The family yielded that bed for my mother and me.

We were confined in a tight space inside the house, but the front yard was huge. People of the family used the front yard as a place to dry the newly harvested rice. The kitchen was on the other side of the front yard in a separated clay range house. This house was framed by bamboo and patted with clay mixed with straw. The roof of the house was thatched with dried palm leaves. The house was divided into two separated compartments with a small opening connecting the two sides. The smaller compartment was used to tie the water buffalo of the family. The larger compartment was used as a place for cooking. Another small opening to the large compartment was used for people to get in to do their cooking. There was another bigger opening to the small compartment used for the water buffalo to get in to rest inside its place.

    Water was provided from a well at a far corner of the front yard. Next to the well was a rectangular concrete water container. They collected rain water and sometimes water from the well in this container. After the water in this container was aged, people used this water for cooking and drinking. There was no faucet or tap water in the village; people used either rain or well water only. There was no bath room here either; everyone would take shower in the open space by the side of the well with the well water. They usually did that at nighttime when it was dark outside; sometimes, the women took shower with their cloths on. Not too far from the well were a large chicken coop and a pig stable, the family raised a lot

Life in the Countryside

of chicken in the coop and several large pigs in the stable. Walking pass the furrows of vegetables to the front edge of the garden was a large fish pond; fresh water fishes were raised in the pond as food for the family. Far from the fish pond at the other side of the garden was a small bamboo frame house which was covered with some simple wattles and was used as a rest-room.

Country life was totally new and excited to me. At early dawn, people waked up very early when they heard the cock-crow while it was still dark outside. Adult people of the family carried their tools along with their water buffalo to the paddy fields at a separate open area near the village. The young girl was staying at home; the first thing she would do was going to the chicken coop and opened its gate for the chickens. Once in a while she would feed the chickens at the front yard of the house, but most of the time, the chickens would wander inside the garden looking for their own food in the ground. The pigs would not have the freedom as the chickens. People of the family would prepare the food for the pigs and would feed them inside the stable. In the evening, before night fall, the chickens would all come back to the coop by themselves before someone would close the gate again.

I did not know if there was any school for

the children in the village. I did not see anyone going to or back from school; all the kids were just playing at home near their houses while their parents were working. Not like our city kids, most of them were illiterate. Their clothing was older and dirtier than of the city kids. They made up their own games to play with each other, boys and girls usually played separately. Next to the property of the family was a large open play-ground. The boys often came out there and played their horse-riding game. They would divide themselves into two separated groups. The bigger boys would carry the smaller boys on his back, and the two groups would start from the two lines at a distance and would charge at each other. They tried to pull at each other until all the boys riding on the other boys' back of one group had fallen down; the group with anyone left riding would win. The girls were usually fond of skipping, rope jumping, or some other feminine type of games with one another at a separated corner.

After staying around the house for a few days, I went out to the play-ground to play with the boys of the village. The first time I went out there, the country boys were mocking me for I was new and looked a little different from them; I was more pale and dressed cleaner than the village boys. I did not like their demeanors toward me and thought they were just jealous with me for I looked better than them. Although I despised them for they were illiterate and not very civilized, I asked if I could join in to play with them. There was one boy, who was a little older among the boys, came and pushed me.

"You look weak; I think you are not fit to play our game", he said.

I thought that despicable, dirty, illiterate boy had nothing better than me, and I was mad. I pushed him back. All the other boys standing around looked at two of us and one boy said "let's fight and see who is stronger". That was how I got into a fight with the older boy. After watching us fight for a while, other kids pulled us apart. When I got home that day, my mother saw the bruises on my face and found out that I was involved into a fight. She kept me at her sight and not allowed me to go outside to play with the other kids in the village anymore.

Staying around the house was so boring; I really wanted to go outside playing as all the other boys of the village and exploring life of people living in the countryside. In the afternoon, after the adult people got home from working in the paddy, the boys in the village would ride on the back of their family water buffalos to tend the animal and let them feed ing off the wild grass at the field. On the hot days, the boys would invite one another to go swimming or fishing at the nearby lake. It seemed that the kids were having a lot of fun. I really liked to ride on the back of the animal or to go swimming as the other boys did. After being kept at home for a while, I begged my mother for her permission to go tending the buffalo with the boy of the family. I promised her that I would not get into any fight with anyone anymore. My mother realized that I was not happy around her all the time and felt pity for me, so she asked Tan, the boy of the family, to keep an eye on me and let me go tending the water buffalo with him.

Tan let me rode with him on the back of his water buffalo. I was scared to jump on the animal's back, but with Tan's help, I got on and sat behind Tan, holding tightly on him. The animal was so big and strong; with both of us sitting on its back but I did not feel our weight affecting the animal at all. It walked slowly and very gentle as we rode on the dirt roads that weaved through the open plain. We both just sat on the back of the animal, chatting with each other, enjoyed the cool breeze and the view of those wide open fields while the animal was eating the wild grass along the way. I had read about the enjoyment of riding the water buffalo in the elementary school book before, but that was the first time I personally rode the animal and I was so delighted.

After that day, I went with Tan on his buffalo out to the fields in most of the afternoons and on the weekends. While we were both sitting on the back of the buffalo, Tan was always the one who guided the animal. Every time he wanted the animal to go forward, he would kick his feet back to the side of the animal, and used the rope which tied to the animal's nose to control the direction. The buffalo understood well and obeyed tan's command very docilely. I just sat behind Tan and enjoyed the ride.

A time when we were arriving at the open field and saw some other boys were playing out there, we both got down from the back of the buffalo and Tan tied his buffalo to a tree so he could join in with those boys. After Tan played with them for a while, the kids ran to the other side of the village and Tan wanted to follow them. He asked me to take his buffalo home for him. After he ran off, I untied the rope from the tree and pulled the buffalo. The buffalo did not follow me as it did with Tan; it just looked at me without moving at all. I pulled a little harder and the animal charged at me. I dropped the rope and ran away until the animal had stopped. I thought that I had either pulled the animal to hard or because I was too nervous and had frightened myself out of my wits; the animal should follow me had I pulled the rope gentler. I came back to pick the rope up. As I just held on the rope, the animal charged at me again. I was really scared this time; I dropped the rope and ran. The water buffalo did not chase me but stopped and went on feeding again. I did not expect that behavior from the gentle animal. I felt helpless and worried that the animal might run away and I was responsible for the loss. I looked for help and fortunately saw a small village boy was playing in a distance. I approached him and asked for help.

The boy just took a small bamboo branch with a lot of leaves from a nearby hedges and walked to the buffalo. He held the rope with one hand and the bamboo branch with other hand in front of the animal. The tender bamboo leaves must be the favorite food of water buffalos, the animal followed him docilely. He walked to Tan's home and the animal followed him. When we got to Tan's house, he tied the animal to its place and threw the bamboo branches down for it. I was amazed by the calmness of the little boy and so thankful of him for his wise and brave action. I had had some grudge and disdain toward the country boys, especially after the fight with one of them; however, from that day, I felt much better and started to like the kids at the village. They might be illiterate but in fact they knew and had something that I lacked and had to learn a lot from them.

After my mother had seen me getting along well with the village boys, she allowed me to go out and playing with other kids with or without the accompanying of Tan. When we were not tending the buffalo, we would go fishing or bird hunting. We made up our own catapults with some rubber bands and some forks of the small Y-shaped branches as our bird hunting equipments. It took a lot of practice before I was able to master the hand-made-hunting-equipment to enjoy the bird hunting with Tan. I also loved to fish with Tan at his family pond. We had some playing cards that I had bought with me from the city. While waiting for the fish to bite the baits, we could play cards and eating the roasted sweet potato that we dug right at his family garden. To roast the sweet potato, we just needed to gather a small pile of hay and burned it. Then we put some potato into the burning hay and left it there. After the all the hay was burned, the potato usually cooked. When we were tired, we would crawl into the big haystack at the corner of the yard to take a nap. It was very comfortable lying inside there; it was cool during the hot day and warm in a cold or windy day.

Another time I went with the village boys to a nearby lake. It was a hot day and the boys jumped down to the water near the bank to play. The water was not deep near the bank. The kids were standing at the area that the water only reached up at their chest or neck high. They ducked down to catch the small fishes or shrimps and held in their months. When they got up, they released them in a bowl floating on the surface of the water. Although I did not know how to swim but the kids were having so much fun so I jumped down and played with them too. I tried to catch the fish as they did but it was not easy. I asked for help and one boy showed me how to do it. They first ducked down at the bottom and used their feet and hands to feel the fishes. The fishes were scared by their movement and looked for some place to hide. Some of them would slip their head into the small shallow holes at the bottom and would not swim away. We could feel the fish with our hand and could catch them. After practiced for a while, I also caught a small fish and put it into the bowl; I was very excited with my first catch.

After catching some small fishes, I stretched my feet out at the bottom to feel another hole and was slipped out to the deeper area. It was very close to the previous spot but I could not land my foot back to the shallow area again. I exerted all the strength of my hands and tried to swim back to the shallow but was getting farther and father and my head started to sink down passing my nose. I tried to call for help but the water was getting into my mouth and could not do it; I was choked with the lake water. Very fortunate, a boy from the closest distance turned and saw me as I was struggling in the water and realized the dangerous situation. He swam toward me, reached out, and pulled me back to the shallow water. After coughing off the lake water, I could breathe normal again and started calming down. After a moment of calmness, I realized the boy who just saved my life was the very boy that I had fought with the first few days after arriving to this village. I was so thankful for his generous action and felt shameful for what I had thought of him previously.

I went home that day and did not tell my mother what had happened to me at the lake. I was afraid my mother would not let me going out again. Perhaps my father had learned some astrology when he was alive; I recalled my father had once told me that according to my horoscope, it would be very dangerous for my life if I play near the water before my teenage years, especially at the age of twelve; I was exactly twelve years old that year.

I thought that my unlucky moment had passed and decided to learn to swim by myself. A few days after the incident, I went back to the lake with the village boys. Instead of catching fish with other kids, I practiced swimming at the area of shallow water. I stood at the area where water only reached my chess. I held my breath and put my face down to the water and swam calmly toward the bank. When I could not hold my breath any longer, I stood up and breathed. After I did that a few times, I realized my body did not sink down and I could turn my face up out of the water to breathe. I knew how to swim since then.

I went swimming at the lake on most of the hot days. The lake was part of the main river and the water at the lake was clean, also there was no leech at the lake. I rarely go down to the water at the paddy fields because I did not like being attached by the leeches. I recall a time I was walking on a small dirt road by the paddy fields with my bare feet and stepped on some wet mud and the mud stuck into my toes. When seeing a ditch near the paddy fields and the water inside the ditch was clear, I deepened my foot down into the water to shake off the wet mud. As soon as the water was stirred, so many long and skinny creatures swam quickly toward my foot from all direction. I looked down closer to see what they were; right at that time I heard a boy standing next to me yelled "leeches, leeches". I immediately pulled my foot out of the water. I looked down at my wet foot and saw a leech already attached to my ankle. I was so scared and kicked my foot up and down but the leech did not fall off. The boy took a dried palm leaf on the ground and scraped the leech off my foot. The blood leaked out for a while at the spot that the leech had attached at my ankle before it stopped. Since that day, I tried to avoid getting down to the paddy water whenever I could. I had wondered what would happen to the people working down at the paddy fields. Later on, I noticed that people working inside the paddy wore some special clothings at their feet which looked similar to the long socks to protect them from the leeches.

There was no electricity at all the country areas far away from town. It was very dark outside at night when there was no moonlight. Some nights there were a lot of fire flies twinkled in the air above the ground. It was very pretty looking out at the field in those dark nights. Tan sometimes invited me to go fire-flies-catching right at the front yard area or in the garden outside his house. We used a piece of cloth from an old mosquito-net and made a small net for ourselves. Using the net, some night we could catch so many fire flies in one night. We would put all the fire flies we caught into a small glass jar to make our fun special lamp. Our fire-fly-lamp could be used for our fun activity such as playing card at night, but it would only twinkle for a while before it died out.

Living in the countryside was fun; especially we did not have to worry about bombing attack. The only one thing that I did not like about country life was using the rest-room at night. The rest-room was so far away from the house. If we needed to use the rest-room at night, we would use a small kerosene lamp

My Adventure to The New World

to see our way in the dark. While holding the lamp in our hand, we had to walk all the way to the corner of the garden where the rest-room was located. I was afraid of the dark, also there were a lot of mosquitoes outside at night; therefore, I would always try my best to delay my personal activity until the next day, but at times it was very uncomfortable. Other than the problem of using the rest-room at night, daytime activities in the countryside were fun.

I was young and had not realized that my mother had been dreadfully worried about our family financial status since the time we left our home. We had not had any income since the time of the evacuation. My brothers were living with some of our friends in the city and they came to see us every week. Every time they came, they always bought food for my mother and me. After months of living in the country side, one day my oldest brother came visiting us and informed my mother that the bombing in the city was over and we all could move back home. I remember my mother was so happy with the good news that day. Right the next day, she met with the family owners to thank them again for our stay and packed up our stuff to go back home in the city. All my brothers also came that day and helped us moving back home.

12. Return to City

In the beginning of 1973, although the Vietnam War was not over yet, the city bombing had finally stopped. Many families in our neighborhood slowly moved back to their homes. It was happy to see everyone coming back to the neighborhood again. All my brothers and sister, except one brother still in the army, moved back home with us. Our family together with our neighbors cleaned up all the debris inside the duplex building. Even though there were still a huge holes at the roof and on every floor of the town house, people just covered the holes on their floors with some wood planks and managed to live while waiting for people to fix them.

One family on the third floor of the town

house had moved away during the bombing evacuation and was not coming back. But the city official arranged three other families, whose homes had been destroyed during the bombing, to move in and lived up there. They divided the room into three sections for the three families. The duplex became even more crowded. Many buildings around our neighborhood were either damaged or destroyed. Some building had only half of it left standing on the foundation; however, people had no place to live so they were managing to live in left over part of the buildings. For those families whose house had been totally destroyed, the city arranged some of them to share room with other families.

Daily life activities in the city returned back to normal and somewhat hastier; everyone was excited and seemed more active than the time before the evacuation. Right after we had settled back home, our family went back to the church to attend Masses as our normal activities again. Every time I went to church, I always looked for Bien, the friend I had left before our evacuation from the city, but I could not find him around the church ground anymore. I thought that Bien's family had also moved out of the city and was not coming back yet, but from someone at the church, I found out later that Bien was dead. He had died not from bombing but from drowning. I was shocked when I learned about the bad news. I recalled Bien's family was living in an area without any river or lake nearby. But he had had a cramp while playing in a very shallow lagoon close to his home and had been drowned. Life is so fragile! I lost a close friend not from the violent war but just a simple cramp. After coming back to our city and when I came to the church ground, I often missed Bien very much, at times I missed him so much that I bought a cigarette and smoked alone at some place that Bien and I had been sitting with each other before to commemorate our dearly bygones. I became a smoker since then.

After we moved back into our duplex, cockroaches were everywhere, especially in the back yard and the kitchen areas. Sometimes they flew into our living rooms and got into our closets and laid their egg on our clothes. We had to use a lot of the naphthalene balls and put them in our closet to prevent them from living in there. During those days, almost every family in our duplex had a small hen-coop in the common kitchen area to raise one or two chickens as food for the Lunar New Year celebration. At night, we could use fly-swatter to swat the cockroaches and collected a full can of them to feed the chickens the next day. The chickens loved to eat cockroaches and would grow very fast if were fed with cockroaches regularly. Also after the evacuation, our building became the good living place for rats. They probably came from other destroyed buildings and hided in the back area of our building.

At times the whole neighborhood got together and organized the rat-killing nights. We would wait until midnight, and then all of us would get inside the kitchen area on the second floor where the rat usually came at night, and then we would close the door of the room. We set a simple trap by the door in front of a big hole at the bottom of the door. Everyone used the metal pokers, which were the tools for the daily work at charcoal ovens, to scare the rats out of their hiding places. When the rat was scared, it would run to the hole at the bottom of the door trying to escape down stairs and to the back of the building. At that time a person, standing one foot on the top part of the charcoal oven by the side of the door, would trample the trap down onto the rat with his other foot. Once the rat was trapped, we all used the sharp metal pokers to kill that rat and put it in a place. We then repeated the process again. One night we caught and killed fourteen big rats in that kitchen alone.

The schools had been reopened and I was going back to school again. After moving away and could not continue our screw galvanizing business, we lost the business contract. Instead of helping my brothers in their galvanizing business, I then had a new heavier chore at home, and that was getting the water for our family daily use. The water piping system to all the buildings in our area was very old. After the bombing, it was totally ravaged. In the beginning after coming back home, we had to go to the Tam Bac River to get river water to use. We filled our water containers with the river water. Then we used alum to precipitate the dirt articles and waited until all the sediments settled at the bottom. The clear water then was used for our daily cooking. After a while, the water company set up the public faucet at the corner of the block. Each afternoon, I would carry two large water buckets to the public water faucet to obtain water for our family.

There was one public water faucet in a corner of the streets for every four blocks in the area; therefore, the line of empty buckets at that place was very long. Everyday in the afternoon, I brought my two large empty buckets and placed them in the long line and waited for my turn. When it was my turn, I filled them, put them on the shoulder-piece, and carried them home. Our living room was on the second floor and I could not use the shoulder-piece on the stairs. So I had to carry each bucket up one by one and filled all the water containers in our back yard on the second floor. I was a small person and not strong enough to carry the full bucket straight all the way up. I just lifted one heavy bucket with both hands one step at a time and that took me almost the whole day to fill all our containers. I used to blame that carrying the heavy water buckets was the main reason had prevented me from growing taller. For that, getting water from the public faucet was my most disliked daily activity. At times I wished that I was older so I could move away from home. After spending a lot of time out on the street with other people around the neighborhood in the same situation, I got use to it and felt more comfortable later on.

My brothers were looking for jobs but could not find any; no one in our family was working and our family financial status was in tight situation again. Not able to get a job, my brothers had tried to launch some other businesses on their own, but they were not successful. It just cost our family even more. We had to economize our daily spending on our family saving and hoped for any new opportunity. Breakfast was removed from our family daily meals except for me since I was the youngest and had to walk to school every morning and would not get home until afternoon; of course, the school was not providing meal in Vietnam as here in the States. One of our new neighbors, who had moved in and was living in our building after the bombing

Return to City

evacuation, hard-boiled sweet potatoes and sold them in our home street as breakfast for poor people. She always woke up around 3 in the morning to cook her sweet potatoes and had them ready everyday by 6 o'clock, right at our kitchen area. My mother often bought some cheap cooked sweet potatoes from her for me as my breakfast.

Although we lived in the tough condition, I was too young at the time to worry about our family day to day problem. After finishing all the family chores and my school work, I just went out playing with some other kids in our neighborhood. All the families in our neighborhood were not in any better situation than ours, but the kids were unaffected by it and still played happily and naturally everyday with one another.

It was the year 1975. I remember clearly that day I was playing cards with some kids inside our neighbor's room down stair and we heard the radio announcing the victory news of the North Vietnamese Deliberation Army on some cities of the South Vietnam. In the beginning we all thought that it would be the same as the other exaggerated news that we had heard before and did not pay much attention to it. But then more news of victories on the other cities came, one after the other. We all stopped playing and listened to the ra-

My Adventure to The New World

dio and were very excited. Then we heard the big news that the Deliberation Army was taking control of Saigon City, the capital of South Vietnam then. Finally the announcement that the whole nation was reunited arrived. It happened so quickly and surprised everyone of us. We all jumped up and down, and ran down to the streets.

On the streets, many kids from other houses were also coming out shouting to rejoice with the victorious news. The next day the local city official announced that every household should hang the Vietnam National Flags in the front area of their houses. Vietnamese people had lived in the war for so long and everyone was so excited that the war was finally over. That year, all major cities in North Vietnam organized the huge Fire Work Festival on the New Year's Day as the first year of the United Vietnam under the new administration. At the night of the Fire Work Festival, some of my friends and I went all the way to the top of the bell tower in the cathedral to watch the fire work. That was the first time I saw so much fire work instead of the firing from the air defense artilleries over the sky of our city.

My oldest brother had always wanted to visit the South. When he was about seventeen years old, he had followed someone trying to escape to the South but had not succeeded. He together with the other people had been caught by the North Vietnam Border Patrol at the Demilitarized Zone. Since he was under eighteen years old at the time, after retaining him for a while, they released him then.

Right after the Vietnam War was over for just a few months, he asked my mother for her permission and the money for him to visit the South. We also had a few relatives living in the South and my brother used our relative visiting as the reason for the trip. Despite our tight financial situation, my mother always cherished my brother and somehow she conformed to his begging. She made every effort and gathered enough money for him to go with hope that he might bring back some new business idea for the family. Right after he got the money, my brother obtained the train ticket and travelled south with a couple of his friends.

For a long time without any news or information from him, my brother came back home almost a year later after visiting many different places in the South and spending all his money. Despite that he had been away from home for that long, he did not bring back any present from the South for anyone in our family, he only brought back a large AKAI tape recorder. My mother was not interested in that luxurious instrument and she was disappointed for he did not even bring back a pair of new shoes for me for I was the youngest boy in the family and not having even a pair of shoes then. But I was very please to see the new musical instrument that he bought back. That kind of musical instrument had not been available in North Vietnam and that was the first time I saw the tape recorder. I was curious and intrigued by the large roll of tapes he bought back with the instrument. More than that, his present for us was those stories from all the places in Saigon City that he had stayed to amuse with his friends and the information of how much better the life of the people living in the South were. I was amazed by all the information that he brought back.

Everynight when he turned on the tape recorder with the love songs written by the South Vietnamese, the music was so different from the songs I had heard from our public radio in the North. All the songs written in the North had been censored by the government and were more about motivating people working in the fields or factories, the soldiers in the battle field, or to praise the leaders of our government. But the songs recorded in the tapes he brought back from the South were more about boy-girl loves, the lost love between lovers and the suffering of the Vietnamese people during the wartime. The music sounded sad and very touchy, and some songs had moved us into tears.

Although the war was over, people's lives were not getting any better. The situation of our family was getting worse and worse. The Vietnamese did not use the banking system back then, people either saved cash or gold and hided it in someplace at their home. I never ask my mother about our family saving, but I thought we had depleted all the gold that our parents had saved since the colonial time when they still having the grocery distributing business. My second brother was also released from military service after the war by then. He came back home and could not find any work for himself either. Our daily life was getting tighter and tighter.

It was very hot during the summer time and no family in North Vietnam had air conditioner or refrigerator then. People often bought ice from the some public store to make cold beverage at home and it was not very convenience. One of my brothers came up with a new business idea; he bought a small ice-making machine from someone who just brought it back out from the South, and we made ice cubes at home to sell to the people in our neighbors. However, the money we made from selling ice cube was too little and not enough to support the whole family; people only needed ice in the summer time. It was actual our family toughest economic time a couple of years after the war. I remember by that time I was a teenager and loved to play soccer but we could not afford a simple rubber ball. Every time I passed by the public sport store in town, I could not resist the attempt to come in to look at the soccer balls in the store with the strong craving for one of them.

As our Vietnamese tradition, on the Lunar New Year Festival, people would give their children some money as the way of congratulation for the kids new age and wishing them a happy New Year (Vietnamese count their age at the Lunar New Year's Day). I saved all that money my mother and other adults gave me on the New Year Festival. After the festival, I went to the sport store and bought me a rubber ball. The amount of money I had was only enough for me to buy a cheap one. The ball was a Made-in-Vietnam ball and was of very poor quality. The thickness of the rubber was not even; therefore, when it was inflated, some areas on the ball protruded out more than other. The ball was not in a sphere shape but deformed and was funny looking, but that was my very beloved toy then.

Everyday in the afternoon around 5 o'clock, with my soccer ball, I went to the soccer field near the city center. The whole city only had one public soccer field. The surface of the field was not cover by grass but just bare dirt. But playing in there was much safer than playing on the street. Shoes were a luxurious items that only the "imperial kids" had; we played with our bare feet. Running bare feet on dirt surface was much softer than on asphalt; the asphalt surface on the street was also very hot in the afternoon in summer time. The ball I had was deformed and would not roll in any certain direction which made our game even more challenging. There was one soccer stadium in the city with grass field, but that stadium was reserved for professional soccer matches only. The city professional soccer team also practiced at the same dirt field since it required little or no maintenance.

One time I went to the soccer field with my soccer ball but it was a crowded day and the whole field was taken, the city soccer team was practicing on the field that day. After my friends and I waited at the field and could not get any area to play our game, we decided to play right at the City-Opera-House not too far from there. The large area in front of the Opera House was also of asphalt surface as on the surface of the streets but it had less traffic there. While we were playing at the square, I kicked at the ball and my toes hit the hard surface on the ground. Ouch! It was so painful. One of my toe nail fell off. Blood was all over my foot. After the injury I could not continue playing soccer for a long time. It was hard for me just to sit by the outside and watch my friends playing so I started to learn to play ping pong after that.

There were a few cement ping pong tables near my house. After the war, the city filled all the zigzag trenches and the bunkers in the ground and set some cement ping pong tables at the open area as a public playing ground. I often came to watch people playing in the area; some of them were very good with the game and often played for money. When the cement table was available, my friend and I used a few bricks that fell out from the ruined building and put them at the middle of the table as our table-net. I cut a piece of plywood into a round shape with a handle and used it as my racket. Even the ping pong ball was not easy for us to get at that time so we took turn to use the ball of each other. We took very good care of our ping pong ball. If the ball was stepped on by accident and was deformed, we would put it into hot water to restore it to the possible original shape and used it until it was totally broken. After I played with my plywood racket for a while, I was getting better at the game and really wanted to have a real racket with the rubber pad on to play with. But even a simple ping pong racket was a luxurious item for us. I wanted to ask my mother for some money to buy a cheap racket, and I was waiting for a right moment to ask her for it.

It was our tradition that the children would get some new cloth to wear on the New Year Festival. One time, it was close to the end of the year and I had out grown all my pants but my family could not afford any new fabric to make me a pair new trousers then. My mother called me in to try on a pair of my father's left over trousers. Most of my father's cloths had been stitched during the colonial time but were of quality materials and still good. When I was by her side, she handed me the pair to try on.
"You are the lucky one since all your brothers had grown taller than your dad and could not fit these anymore." She grinned.
I tried them on but they looked very funny on me; they were too long and the waist size was too big that I had to hold them at the waist with my hands to prevent them from falling down. I laughed as I pulled the pair of trousers up close to my chest. She also smiled but then I saw she was blinking her eyes. I did not know if she was thinking about my deceased father or about the deprivation of our life at the time. I looked at her and saw some tear came out from her eye. I felt a glancing sadness and tried to cheer her up.
'This is not too bad mom; you can fix them for me.'

I said and took off the pants and gave them to her so she could alternate them for me. As she was working on them, I recalled those stories from my brother after his visiting trip to the South and how better life had been in there. I asked:

'Mother, I heard that life of people in the South had been much better than here in the North, is that right?'

My mother pulled out a handkerchief and gently wiped her eye. She smiled and said softly:

"Probably there had been more freedom in there and people had been allowed to work freely on their own businesses. When people work for themselves, they would work harder; perhaps when everyone in the whole society is working harder, life of the society as a whole wuold be better."

I waited for her to finish and asked again:

'Why you did not move to the South in 1954 when we were free to choose which side to live?'

My mother thought that I was reproaching her for the bad decision, she slowly replied:

"When the country was just divided into two sections and people were free to choose which side to reside, I also wanted to move to the South but your father decided not to. He said that our homeland had just become independent and we should stay to contribute our help to rebuild it. I insisted on moving to the South and had tried to change his mind but I could not change his decision then. The spirit of our people after the victory at Dien Bien Phu battle was very high then. At that time, the victorious songs and the promise of a free and better life for all people were broadcasted everyday on the radio of the newly established government. Several of your father's old friends who had jointed the revolution came back and stayed at our home to party with him everynight. They all were confident in the Revolution and that made your father believed strongly in the new administrator; however, most of his friends had been left unused by the new government later on. One day your father took me to see 'The Little Hero Le Van Tam Drama', the patriotic boy who had poured gasoline on his clothes and then lit up his body to use himself as a live torch and ran into the French barracks to blow up the enemy's ammunition depot. Your father wanted me to see how much our people had sacrificed for our independence and tried to change my opinion. But after seeing the show, I wanted to move to the South even more; I sensed something very bad would happen to our family. I told your father that nationalism was only the political boundary which had been created by adult people; the boy was innocent and had not had sufficient wit to decide for himself; someone must either enticed or coerced him to do that devilish act. Although I had tried to convince him to move to the South but you know that once your father had decided, he would not change his mind."

'So that was why we did not move?' I asked.

As soon as I fished my last word, she looked straight at me and in a deliberately manner, she said a Vietnamese idiom:

"Tai gia tong phu, xuat gia tong phu, phu tu tong tu."

(The Vietnamese idiom means: while living with the parents, girls should follow the parents; after marriage, they should follow their husbands; after their husbands died, they should follow their sons)

My mother had been ingrained deeply with our old tradition. Like most other Vietnamese women at her contemporary, she had always stood sacrifices and hardships for the family. I was attempting to ask her for some money to buy a new ping pong racket, but feeling for her situation, I never ask her for it again.

After the war was over, the city built a new middle school right in a bombed-ruined area near our house. I was in the fifth grade and was transferred to that new school; it was so close that it only took me less than five minutes to walk there (I lost a couple of years without schooling due to the war). I was happy with my new school since most of my new friends were living near my neighborhood. In my class I had a new good friend named Van. Van was a couple of years older than me and was a tall and skinny boy. He was a nice and polite person but most of the time he did not turn in his homework on time. He often asked me for help with his math homework. I once asked him why he did not do his home work at home, and he told me that he had to work and make some extra money to support his family.

One Friday after school, Van invited me to come with him to his house. His family lived in a neighborhood on the other side of the Tam Bac River not too far from my house. From our school, we walked pass my house and then across the suspension bridge to the other side of the river. After passing the bridge, we turned left and walked by the river bank to his home. Van' family lived in a very poor housing area right by the river. When we got to his house, the house was not even locked and no one was home. There were only some old and simple furniture inside the living area. The house was almost empty and was constructed by several galvanized sheets right on the earth floor near the river bank. While I was with him, Van asked me if I want to make some money with him. I asked him how but he did not explain, he just said that I should be at his place at five o'clock the next morning. I was curious and also wanted to have some money to buy a new ping pong racket, so I accepted his invitation.

The next morning, I woke up very early and ran to his house. When I got there, Van was already up and waited for me by the door on the outside of his home. Without saying a word, he took a plastic basin in the front yard and handed me an empty bucket. He got back inside and took out a long pole and held it with his other hand. I was curious and looked at the pole on his hand. It was a long dried bamboo branch with the length of two of my body heights. At the end of it, Van tied a metal wire shaped like a letter T. I pointed at the pole and asked him:

'What is that?'

Van kept on walking and did not answer my question. With a secrete look, he said:

"Just follow me."

I carried the bucket and followed him. Van walked so fast that I had to run sometimes to be at his side. We walked across the bridge on the Tam Bac River and then pass my house to the Lap River on the other side of the two blocks.

Lap River was called a river but a portion of this river had been filled up and became part of the city park. Only the left over section still connected to the main stream and that was why it had the name Lap (filled) River. The edge of the river was curbed with stone walls down to the bank to make the river looked neat and clean. However, people with low sense of responsibility had littered their trash into the river. Therefore, after a long period of time, the river bank had become muddy and the portion of the river near the filled area was very shallow.

When we were at the river, Van slipped on the rock-wall down to the bank with his tool and the basin. Once he has reached the bank, he signaled with his head to ask me to get down with him. It was very dirty down there so I hesitated a little but got down anyway. Van asked me to sit at the bank near the water with the bucket and waited for him. He waded a few steps into the river with the basin in one hand and his tool on the other. With the basin floated on the water surface, he held onto it and swam with his feet toward the middle of the river. I sat and watched as he was getting farther from the bank. The water of the river was very cold in the morning; I didn't know what Van was trying to do but I felt anxious and worried for him.

When Van was at the middle of the river, he stretched out and deepened his pole deep into the water with one of his hand. Once the pole and his hand were deep in the water, he pulled his tool and slowly lifted it up out of the water. He then plucked off the mud that tucked at the T shape wire into the basin. He repeated that action over and over. By that time, I started figuring out what Van was trying to do. After a while, he swam back toward me at the bank. When he was close, he pushed the floating basin toward me and asked me to dump the mud inside the basin into the bucket and gave the empty basin back to him. With the empty basin on the water surface, he swam back to the middle of the river to do the same thing again.

    I sat there wondering how Van would filter out this muddy stuff, but I did not have to wait too long. After about ten minutes, I looked back at the bucket; I saw some small red spots at the surface of the mud. I looked closer and realized that the red spots were created by a lot of tiny blood-worms. After a short quiet moment, the worms in the mud came to the surface and rolled into one another. In about three hours, the bucket was almost full, Van got out of the water and we both went back to his home. At his home, Van poured the mud in the bucket down at his yard and cleaned up his equipments.

    We ate lunch from some left over food of his family. After lunch, Van took a small empty can to the mud that he had poured down his yard. Using his hand, he scooped up a large and a few small clots of blood-worms and put them into the empty can. We took the can full of blood-worms to the tropical fish store in town. The proprietor of the store had often bought the worm from Van and knew him well, so they did not have to negotiate about the price for his worms. As Van handed him the can of worms, the proprietor took the can to the back room and came out with some money and gave it to Van.

After selling the blood-worm, Van showed me all the money we just made and gave me my share. That was the first time I made some money by myself and it was a proud feeling, but somehow I felt bad for Van. It was very hard and could be dangerous work but the money Van made that day probably was not enough to buy one day food for his family.

After I told my mother how I was helping Van to collect the blood worms and about the money he had gave me, my mother did not allow me to do that anymore. She found out that I was saving some money to buy a ping pong racket so she gave me some and made sure that I promised her not going to work with Van anymore. With all the money I had, I was able to buy me a cheap ping pong racket with the rubber pads on both sides of the racket to play with.

My Adventure to The New World

13. The New Business

The daily life of the people in general was getting harder and harder. When our family was in a desperate situation, one of our relative came out to the city to visit and stayed with us. He was a good-natured country man in his fortieth and he called my mother aunty. People in his village was specialized in making fake paper flowers and had been making their living by producing the paper flowers and selling them at the cities by the end of each year. After staying with us for a while, he recognized our financial difficulty and suggested that he would help our family to produce paper flowers for sale at the Lunar New Year's Festival. He was willing to stay and lived with us the first year to show us where to obtain the materials and step by step in the process of how to produce the flowers.

There were many steps involved in making the flowers and it would take us almost the whole year of production. First the special dies, the papers, several different color dyes, and all other necessary materials were procured. The paper we used to make flower were of special kind and must be either clear or white. We dyed many stacks of papers with different colors and let them dried naturally. The dies were used to cut each stack of dried color papers into the shapes of petals and leaves. After having the leaves and petals, thin stacks of petals were curved at the edges to imitate the genuine flower petals. The petals were then rolled into the end of a small piece of wire about a span long, one by one by hand, with a thin long ribbon of the dyed green paper. Several leaves were attached along the wire while rolling the green ribbon on the wire to make the flower branch. Six or seven small flower branches would then be attached to a thin bamboo rod, about three spans long, with another longer green paper ribbon to make a complete branch of flowers. After each branch was completed, it would be folded flat and stored in the carton boxes until the end of the year. We would sell the flowers at the end of the year before the New Year's Festival.

About two weeks before the lunar New

The New Business

Year Festival, we used wooden pole and coiled a lot of straws at one end of the pole and tied them firmly. We then took each branch of the paper flowers out and reshaped the flowers into the best natural shapes. The flowers looked far from genuine flowers but we intended to sell them at an affordable price for the common people. We stuck the fake flower branches at the end of the poles and brought them to the New Year Flower Market to sell.

At the center of the city was a large City Opera House. The opposite side of the square in the front of the Opera House was a large city park with a few flower booths which were permanently built in there. During the Lunar New Year Festival ("Tet" in Vietnamese), the city allowed people to use part of the city park as the New Year Flower Market.

I was a member of the retail-selling team for our family business. After schooling in the mornings, in the afternoons, I would take the flowers to the market to sell. I was shy at first and tried to avoid all the people that I knew while I was at the market with my flower pole. However, after selling the flowers there for a several days, I got use to it and the time working at the flower market became one of a special and memorable time in my life. During the last two weeks of the lunar year, the downtown area was crowded with shoppers and sellers.

Growers from different villages came to town to sell their home grew flowers too, all kind of flowers. There were also fire work merchants and incense sellers. The emitted fragrance from the seller's burning sample incenses pervaded the whole place. Once in a while, the sound of the fire crackers from the children playing nearby together with the smoke from the fire work combined with the burning incenses made the festival atmosphere of the New Year very unique and hard to describe. I could never forget those memorable days.

We sold each branch of flowers for about thirty to fifty cents; it was less than the cost of a small breakfast at the time. In Vietnam, almost every family has an altar for their ancestors inside their homes. In the first few days of the Lunar New Year, people would decorate the altar with flowers and burning incense. The real flowers would be expensive and did not last very long; therefore, many people chose to buy the affordable paper flower then. We could sell all our flowers in just two weeks before the New Year. The profit we obtained from selling the flowers supported our family for the whole coming year. I also had a lot more money from selling flowers to buy my fire works to play with during the New Year Festival. When the festival was over, we would rest for one or two months before everyone would get back into producing paper flowers again.

Producing and selling paper flowers helped our family passing a few years during the time of tough economy, but then the better quality imitated fabric flowers from China slowly drove us out of business. After making and selling paper flowers no longer brought us enough profit, we had to stop our paper flower business and were again looking for some new thing to do. After a long period of searching, my oldest brother together with his friend came up with a new business idea of making rubber pulley belts. They rented a small place at the industrial area close to my house for the start up of their production and hired my other two brothers to work for them. However, their business was not successful and was shut down after only a few months of production.

After several months of leisured, it was my mother who came up with a new business idea again. At that time, the government pharmacies did not have enough medicine for everyone. Only the people who were working for the government and had the special quota could buy the medicine. My mother bought back the medicines from those people having the medicines but not needing them and resold the medicines in the black market. I was busy with my school work so my teenage sister became the medicine retailer. After buying the medicines, my mother would give them to my sister and my sister would bring them to the street near our house to sell. To sell the medicines, she just sat at the corner of a intersection of the streets near our area with the medicines in a small tray and sold them to those who needed them.

Medicine retailer was not allowed and either the market-control personnel or the police would confiscate all the stuff from my sister if they caught her. Therefore, while sitting with her tray on the street, she always had to be alert and let her eyes wandering around for the market-control personnel or the police. She would carry her medicine tray and run away when seeing them from the distance. In those days, the market-control personnel patrolled the streets everyday and my sister was constantly on the run while out on the streets to sell her stuff and it was very hard for her.

One time she went home with tear in her eyes and my mother asked her what had happened. She burst out crying with bitter tears and said that one market-control officer had taken all her stuff. That day the market-control officer didn't wear uniform; therefore, my sister could not recognize him from afar to run away. He caught her and confiscated all her stuff away. She was left with a piece of paper to give to my mother.

Everything was hard in the beginning, but after that time, she learned and sat closed to the other peddlers on the streets so she could run with them when they saw the market-control personnel.

We were living in narrow circumstance, but we were not the only one, almost every other family was in the same situation at that time. I was unaffected by our circumstance then. I was too young and not thinking much about it. As all my friends, I was a happy student and we still enjoyed those days that our school organized the trips to the countryside to help the farmers working in the fields, usually on the weekends. I did not have a bicycle at that time and had to ride with my classmates on their bicycles. On those labor days, very early in the morning, the whole class would meet in our school before going to a certain village near the city. We would take turn riding each other to those villages to do the labor works. It was hard works but it was fun for all the students then. The only thing that I did not like when we were at the rice fields was the leeches. Some of them were so big that people called them buffalo leeches; perhaps they usually attached to the buffalo's feet. But they could also attach to human feet too. I had seen one about eight inches long.

Before each labor trip, my mother used cooked rice and pressed it into a few rice balls about fist size. She also roasted some sesame and crushed them with salt to make sesame salt. She gave me the rice balls and some sesame salt to use as my lunch for the trip. At the working site, we often helped the farmers in making the canal for the rice fields. At break time, all the students would sit together and sharing lunch with one another; we took turn telling chokes and the funny stories. That was the time for some boys and girls to have a chance to know more about each other and became lovers. After the long hard working day, we would ride each other home on our bicycles late in the afternoon. Everyone was usually very tired but having a lot of fun while biking and laughing together on our way home.

One time when I got home from the trip, I was so exhausted that I could not do anything but lying flat on the floor of our house. My mother saw me so tired, she shook her head and said that our public school had exploited the labor of the young students; I just laughed.

After struggled for a time, my mother obtained some connections from the medicine smugglers. She bought the popular medicine from them and resold it to the retailers in the black market. We had to hide the medicine at our friends' places to avoid the shadowing of the police. When there was a buyer, my mother would ask me to go and get it back for her. The police would search our home and would confiscate everything if they found out we had the stuff at home. I was just a teenager and the market-control personnel would not pay much attention to me. By this time I was given a mini bicycle for the job, which my mother had bought from someone who worked on an oversea cargo ship. That was a used Made-in-Japan bicycle and it was the one thing I was very proud to have. I only used that bicycle mainly for the family business and some special occasions. I used a school bag and put some crumbled paper inside to make it looked as my school books so the market-control personnel would not suspect my activities. They could be anywhere on the streets, so I always had to act well as just any other innocent student. The buying and selling medicine business helped our family with a decent living standard although we were always living in fear that the government would seize our home at anytime those days.

14. The Vietnam-China War

In the beginning of 1978, tension between Vietnam and China was high and Vietnam was again on the brink of war with the giant neighbor nation. After the prolonged Vietnam War and Vietnam had barely united for a few years, Cambodia, under Pol Pot as the General Secretary of the Communist Party of Kampuchea, harassed the southern regions of Vietnam. The Vietnamese Government recruited young men and sent it arm force to invade Cambodia. China had acted as a big brother in the united block of the communism countries in Asia, was not very happy with the Vietnamese military action. The Chinese Government had showed truculence and threatened to attack Vietnam. The Vietnamese Government was preparing to carry out a war of resistance against China. For that, the Chinese Nationals living in Vietnam were suggested and allowed by the Vietnamese Government to go back to China before the explosion of the war between the two countries.

On my home streets, many Chinese Nationals, whose houses had been destroyed by bombing and had had no place to live. The city had constructed a row of bamboo cottages right on the street in front of my house as the temporary places for them to live there. Of course, there was no bathroom or any basic facility in those cottages. The Chinese Nationals living in those uncomfortable cottages went back to China by land first. When they crossed the border, they were forced by the Chinese Government to live and to work with heavy labor in the work-camps or state-run plantations at some remote areas. I learned about their living condition from some of their letters they had sent back to their friends in Vietnam. According to their letters, their lives in China were even worse than when they were still in Vietnam. Almost every Chinese living in China at that time had to dress in one style of clothing with the same light-blue color, no matter that they were in the work-camps, in the factories, or out on the streets. The Chinese Government had controlled their people much tighter than the Vietnamese Government. They did not allow their people to have any kind of opinion of their own; their government required that all Chinese should look the same and should act the same according to their rule. The government disregarded any individual opinion and treated their people with very low or no respect at all. In those work-camps and plantations, people just worked and acted like the robots. There was absolutely no freedom of any kind.

Those Chinese Nationals who had not returned to China by that time were afraid of living in those work-camps in China and trying to delay their repatriation. Then the war exploded at the Vietnam-China Border. The Chinese Government used the human tide of army soldiers to attack all the Vietnamese towns and villages near the border. The main Vietnamese Arm Force was stuck at the Cambodia battle field in the south then, but the Vietnamese regional soldiers at those border villages fought back bravely. The bullets of the local machine guns from the commanding positions in Vietnam side fired uninterruptedly until the guns were out of bullets, but the Chinese soldiers were too many. As soon as the Vietnamese soldiers in a position were out of bullet, the Chinese Army attacked and occupied those positions. The human corpses of the dead soldiers floated all over the rivers and some even drifted down to the nearby area of our home city. I remember by the time I was in the refugee camp in Hong Kong a few years latter, I met a Chinese National, who had gone back to China by land and had been stuck at some Chinese region near the Vietnam-China Border by that time, he told me that during the fierce fighting time at the Vietnam-China Border, he had witnessed daily the long line of many crews of Chinese Army trucks that carried full loads of Chinese soldier corpses back from the border.

In my home town, the children came out and gathered on the streets to play the marching game as a group of people rose up in arms against the oppressive power. With sticks and cans in their hands, they shouted out the name of a Vietnamese hero Le Dinh Trinh, who had recently been killed by the Chinese soldiers at the border. The kids marched on the streets showing fervent hatred toward the invaders. Looking out at the children playing on my home streets, I even saw some teenage girls marching with the boys; at that moment I actually understood why the Vietnamese often say: "giac den nha dan ba cung danh" (The Vietnamese idiom means: When the enemy come to our home, women too will rise up in arms). Seeing the enthusiasm among the young people, I then truly realized what the spirit of a small nation that had been under oppression for too long.

The Vietnam War had been just over for

a couple of years but again Vietnam was immediately involved into the war with its neighbors. My friend from grade school, Van - the one who had worked by collecting blood worm - had not been admitted into high school and had been compelled to join the army. He had lost one of his hands in the Cambodia battle field in the south and had been discharged from the arm force. He was barely eighteen years of age and was already a disable ex-serviceman. Now the Vietnamese again had to fight another war with a huge neighbor nation right next to us in the north. No one knew of how many more young people would die for this war. I remember I had once asked my mother why the Vietnamese have always been living in war and my mother responded in Vietnamese "Ca lon nuot ca be". (Big fish swallows smaller fish - She explained that when mankind's consciousness is still inferior, we would act not much different than the other species.)

By the time the Chinese Invading Army had come close to the major cities of Vietnam, the Vietnamese Ministry of Defense started to move its regular troops from the south to the north battle field. However, the Chinese Army withdrew out of Vietnam by then and China announced that they only wanted to teach Vietnam a lesson.

My Adventure to The New World

15. The First Escape

After the war had exploded at the Vietnam-China Border, the Chinese livings in Vietnam were not able to go back to China by land anymore. The Chinese Nationals were then allowed by the Vietnamese Government to leave the country by sea, and that had created a good opportunity for them to come directly to some other free countries; many Chinese Nationals had decided to sail to Hong Kong - an English territory at that time - by boats. Several families would gather their money and bought a sail-boat to travel together to Hong Kong. The Vietnamese Government didn't like the Chinese leaving the country that way much, it was harder for the government to control, but they rather let them go than keep them inside the country and the government would not detain anyone if he or she was a Chinese National.

In Vietnam, every family had to register with their local district official regarding their family information such as their race, living address, birth day of each member of the family... The district government would then provide a Family Register Book for each family if they were allowed to live in their district. Before leaving the country, the boat owner, who was also a Chinese National, must notify the local police department the time and the boarding location. The police would check the Family Register Book of each family at the boarding site, and if they were Chinese, the police would let them go. We called this "semi-formal departure".

Vietnamese people were not allowed to leave the country. More than that, travelling by sail-boat was slow and dangerous; no motor-boat was available for lay-people in North Vietnam at that time. But some Vietnamese exploited this movement and tried to escape from the country along with the Chinese. Some individuals had connection with the corrupted police officers and organized the escape for other Vietnamese in exchange for gold.

There was a corrupted top range police officer of the city at the time who received money from his lower range personnel and let them

The First Escape

made the fake Chinese National Family Register Book for the Vietnamese who bribed them. Those Vietnamese had to pay a lot of money to obtain the fake Family Register Book to escape with the Chinese Nationals to Hong Kong.

Our home was close to the China Town and there were many Chinese living near our neighborhood. We had heard stories of a few Chinese families whose boats had sunk at sea on the way to Hong Kong and many families had been drowned. Although many people were horrified by the news, my brothers had not been able to find any work for a long time and recognized that travelling with the Chinese Nationals was a new and only chance to get out of Vietnam. They talked to my mother and tried to persuade her into planning for the escape of our whole family. Although my mother was an assertive person, in the beginning, my mother did not accept their risky idea, but as she had been deeply ingrained with the Vietnamese phrase 'phu tu tong tu' (Follow the son after husband died) and always listened to my oldest brother; she somehow yielded to my brother opinion. Finally, my mother decided to take the risk and spent our saving for us to escape Vietnam.

My brother knew a Chinese National who was a boat owner and had the connection with the corrupted policemen to obtained

My Adventure to The New World

the require documents. The payment for each family member was about twenty ounces of gold. That was very valuable at the time and my mother took all our saving and came up with the sufficient amount to pay for the whole family. After we gave that person part of the gold amount, he worked out with the police, and a few weeks later, gave us the fake Family Register Book and informed us about the date of departure. A few days before the departure-day, we would at that time pay him the rest of the gold amount and they would let us know the exact time and boarding location of the trip.

    On the departure night, we locked our house behind us and everyone in our family left our house. No one carry any heavy luggage except a small bag of personal items and some clothes. We did not sell any furniture before our leaving since our departure was illegal and needed to be very secretive. I remember that night the electricity at our area was turned off by the city to conserve energy and it was very dark around the neighborhood. Everyone in our family left home separately to avoid the attention from other people in the neighborhood. There are many river branches in the city. We walked to the boarding site at a river branch far from our home. I walked with my mother and it took us more than an hour to get there.

The First Escape

When my mother and I arrived at the site, I took a glance around the area but it was a very dark night and there was no sight of anyone around; only one or two street lights far away from the site. A sail-boat was docked at a dark spot by the river bank. We walked there and saw a large wood plank set by the side of the boat for people to walk down. After all members of our family met at a place near the site, we started to walk to the boat. There was a person, holding a beam light, stood at one side of the boarding plank to check the number of the boarding persons according to the Family Register Book of each family as we walked down.

As we got down to the boat, there were so many people already down there. The boat was packed with many people sitting inside and there was not any empty space left. It was so dark that I could not recognize who were there. When everyone has board and the boat was ready to depart, I felt suffocated and so nervous. I could not believe the boat owner had planed for us to leave the country to go on a long trip in that condition, but I just kept quiet. Right at that moment, I heard the sound of the automobiles arriving at the site. After that was the sound from the stopping of a large bus very close to the boat. Then two policemen came to the boat. They ordered everyone out on shore.

In the outside area on the river brink, there was a jeep with a man dressed in suit sat imposingly on the passenger seat. Behind the jeep was a large bus. As we came out of the boat, the policemen escorted all of us to the bus. The bus driver was another policeman sitting at the driver seat. When everyone had boarded the bus, one policeman closed the door of the bus and got back to the jeep. Together with the other policemen, they all jumped on the jeep and drove off with the man in suit. The bus driver started the bus and followed them to the main police station.

I found out later, the man dressed in suit was the very top range corrupt police chief that had allowed his followers to make the fake documents for many people. His name was Hoang Tru and was the head of the police department of the whole city. He had not only involved in the making of the fake Chinese National Family Register Books, he had also received a lot of bribe money from smugglers and had covered them from their unlawful business. At that time, private trafficking good between the North and the South was illegal. I heard that some young pretty women had even slept with him so they could be able to do their business illegally and their product would not be confiscated by the market control personnel. After his bribing activity was divulged and he heard

The First Escape

his name was in the rumor, he ordered to arrest of all people in the boat that night, and he himself leaded the other policemen to do the very arrest.

When we got to the police station, the police released all the real Chinese Nationals and only detained the Vietnamese. They confined all adult men in a large detention room without any window in the back of the station. Women and children were confined at another room with a small window out in the front of the station. I was confined with my mother and my sisters in that room. We all just sat on the floor since there was neither chair nor bed in there. If anyone needed to use the bath room, we would ask the guard policeman sitting at the booth near the door not too far from the window and he would escorted that person to the bath room.

I was the only boy sitting in that room with all the women and I knew the police would not do anything to me since I was only a tiny teenager boy. Also, after witnessing the condition of the people inside the boat, I did not feel bad that we were arrested; however, I felt a sharp torment in my gut every time I saw the sadness in my mother's face. The next afternoon, they released all women and children but still confined the men at the station.

My mother and I, together with my sisters, went home and everything was the same as nothing had happened to us. It seemed that our neighbors had no idea about what had happened to our family. We got back to our normal daily activities as usual.

About two weeks after our family unsuccessful escape, one afternoon, I was standing at our balcony and looking down to the street, I saw two of my brothers were walking on the street toward our house. Their mustaches had grown long on their faces but they looked very happy. Both of them were smiling while walking fast toward our duplex. I was so happy seeing them coming home, but I wondered what had happened to my oldest brother. He was not coming back with my other two brothers at that time. I ran back in our house and told my mother the good new.

My mother was sitting at her chair, when she heard the news, her eyes turned bright with joy; she stood up and walked toward the door to meet my brothers. As soon as my brothers reached the door, we all walked into our living room and closed the door behind us. My mother asked them what had happened to them during their confinement. My brothers told us about the living condition and what the police had interrogated them while they were confined in the police station. They also told us about what had happened to other people in there. After the interrogation, the police release two of my brothers with other men but retained some men who had previous offence in their record. My oldest brother was still retained for he was the head of our house hold.

The police transferred my oldest brother to Tran Phu Prison located right in the corner of the city, waiting for court trial. On the trial day, he was sentenced for two years of imprisonment. There were two reasons for the court to convict him. The first reason was that he was the oldest man in the family who supported to make all the family decision and the planning for the escape. The second reason was that he had been previously convicted for trying to follow some other people to escape to the South at the time he was about seventeen years old. After the trial day, the police took him back to Tran Phu Prison, and he was confined in there for a while before they transferred him to Hoanh Bo Prison in a remote area of Quang Ninh Province. He had been imprisoned there until his sentence was expired.

The first unsuccessful escape of our family was happening during the summer school vacation. I was in the tenth grade that year and that was the senior year of high school in North Vietnam at that time. Although our escaping attempt was a big financial loss to our family, I was glad that I was still able to be around all my friends.

During the whole grade and high school years, instead of the students leaving the current classroom and coming to the new room for a new subject at each different period, all the students of each class would just sit together in one classroom waiting for the different teachers to come. While waiting for the new teacher, they would have more time playing with each other. For that, the relation-ship of the whole clase was very close. Especially, at the end of the high school years, by then we were mature enough to appreciate our friendship with one another but not old enough to assume the responsibility for our families; therefore, we were unaffected by the family financial burden. That made the bond of the friendship at the end of high school years even stronger.

In school, I had two close friends and we always hung out together as a group. We were so close to one another that we sometimes ate and slept overnight at each other's houses. Our parents treated each one of us warmly as we all were members of the same family and often called us " The Three Musketeers". One person in our group was my very best friend and his first name was Dzung. During my last high school year, I still looked as a young boy with a small body but Dzung was a strong-built-person. When we played soccer at the city soccer field, dogfight often broke out between different groups of players. I was small and sometimes being bullied by other guys. Dzung always protected us from those bully guys if he was with us in the field that day. One of my daily chores was getting water from the public water faucet for my family. When carrying the water bucket up stairs, I had to hold the bucket with both my hands and placed the bucket on each step one at a time. Dzung sometimes came and helped me. He could lift up the heavy water bucket with one hand and carried it straight up stairs without stopping.

Dzung and I often went out with each other at night. We liked to take a long walk with each other as we trolled the city downtown streets. Once in a while we would go to a movie or just sitting at a small tea shop to chat with some other friends. I remember at the end of that high school year, we had a party at one of our friends' house. Dzung and I were both in the party and we both had some alcohol and were a little drunk. After the party was over, everyone left that house and went home; Dzung and I were the last two persons to leave the house and we were walking home very late that night. We could not walk straight and had to hold our hands over each other's shoulders so we would not fall down while walking on the street. We were laughing as we swayed in the quiet night. The stars on the sky that night seamed so bright and the whole starred firmament was so pretty. We both wanted to enjoy the special moment with each other and did not want to go home. When we were at the intersection which separated our ways to each other's house, we did not want to leave each other. Instead of walking on his way home, Dzung walked with me to my house and then turned back to walk alone home. But I also wanted to do same thing for him, so I walked back with him until we both got back to the same intersection again. We were ridiculed by our silly action but really enjoyed the night of our last high school years together. When I got home that day, it was almost dawn. That was the last memorable night I had with a dear high school friend.

At the end of the summer vacation of the high school year, students had to take the college admission exams to be selected into colleges. There were three different exams of different group of subjects. The exam the student would take was depending on which college the student would apply for. Dzung was applying for Marine Science College and I was applying for Marine Navigation since I had always had a dream of sea traveling.

Dzung and I would take the same admission exam which included three subjects:

mathematic, physic and chemistry. Dzung lived about forty walking minutes from my house but I often walked to his house so we could study together for our college admission exam during the last summer break. While I was there, his mother often prepared meals for us eating together at his home and I had regarded his home as my second home.

But my other friend in our group, Dong, chose to become a policeman. I was surprised that Dong had decided to join the Police Force; we normally did not like and sometimes hated the police. But Dong told us that he was the only son in his family and his father had been afraid that he might be mandated to join the army if he was not admitted into any collage and could die in the battle field. His father wanted to make sure that Dong be alive to carry on the lineage of the family.

On the exam taking day, I was inside the class-room working on the exam as all other students; suddenly, the school principal and one policeman came to the room and stood by the door. They signaled the superintendent to come out of the room. In a short moment, the superintendent got back in and asked me to stop working on the exam and came out. When I got out, the principal at the door told me that I was not allowed to take the exam because my family had attempted to escape the country. According to the Vietnamese Government, that was a betraying act to our nation.

I was so sad. I knew that I could finish the exam with high score and had thought that I would be able to enter the college of my dream, it was just my vain dream then. I walked home and told my mother what just happened to me in school. My mother sighed, but then she tried to cheer me up so she said: "van hay chu tot khong bang thang dot co tien". (Which is a Vietnamese idiom means that a rich illiterate guy is better than a poor literate person). I was ridiculed by what she said but could not laugh then.

After the college admission examination, Dzung was admitted to university and was very busy with his school work. My other friend, Dong, was also accepted by the Police Academy and moved out of town to live at the Police Academy Training Camp.

I was left out and be the only person in our group with a boring life and had nothing to do. I just stayed home and helped my mother with her business and the house hold chores when she needed. I had a lot of freetime and once in a while came to Dzung's house, but he was always busy with his school works every time I came. His parents wanted him to focus on studying and seamed not very happy to see him spending time with me. After sensing that, I rarely came to his house anymore.

16. The First Love

After high school years, all my close friends continued the college education and had their girl friends at their college. They were even busier after having their girl friends and we did not have much time with each other anymore. Without any close friend around, life seemed to be boring and I started to feel a little embittered.

With a lot of freetime, I usually came down to the first floor of our town house and chatted with Don, one of my neighbors, although he was about ten years older than me. His father was a tailor and Don worked with his father at home. At that time, the ready-made clothing was not available. People had to bring their fabric to the tailor shop to cut and to have it made there, but new fabric was still a rare material then and the business was not busy; therefore, Don was also free most of the time. We would sit in the front door to play chess or watched people either walked or rode by. The industrial zone on the other side of the Tam Bac River had been active again and the suspension bridge had been repaired, many people were using the bridge and passing by our home street everyday.

There was a young pretty girl walking by our house every afternoon. She was about sixteen or seventeen years old. She always carried a satchel in one hand and her other hand was holding the chin-strap of her wide Vietnamese hat as she walked by our neighborhood. Every time she passed by the tailor shop and saw Don and I were sitting there, she was shy and would tilt her hat toward us to hide her face. Don and I noticed that and paid even more attention to her. Don probably sensed that I liked the girl. One day I was sitting with Don and he defied me to acquaint her. I actually thought about that but I was hesitant and refused to do it. Don tried to talk me into doing it but I kept refusing. Finally, Don said that if I could get her to ride with me on my bicycle, he would pay for a whole night out at what ever restaurant in town I choose.

Although I did not openly accept his

challenge at that time; but then I decided to do it secretly. It was difficult to make friend with a strange young girl on the street. The Vietnamese girls were usually very shy and it was our culture that good family girls would not talk or make friend with strangers out on the streets. From her age and what she often carried with her, I guessed that she was a student of the An Phien High School on the other side of Tam Bac River. I found out that everyday, after school, she had to walk across the suspension bridge on Tam Bac River and passed by my house on her way home. Her home must be far from our area since she had not looked familiar to us.

The next day, I waited until the time she usually walked by. I took my bicycle and waited for her on the other side of the bridge. Since no one was allowed to ride on the small bridge, when I saw her coming, I towed my bicycle and walked toward the bridge as I was just happened to be there by coincidence. I tried to walk close to her and wanted to get some of her attention but she was shy and not looking at me at all. When we were arriving to the other side of the bridge, I said good bye to her and got on my bicycle to ride home as I was just any other passenger.

The next day, I came to the bridge and waited for her again. This time when I met her at the bridge, I said 'hi' to her as I towed my bicycle and walked on the bridge toward her. She smiled softly and nodded her head. I was so happy but was too nervous and could not find anymore word to open our conversation. We were walking by each other on the bridge and I thought she was waiting for me to start the conversation, but I did not know how to start. I kept on walking with her until we were across the bridge, again I said good bye to her and got on my bicycle. This time she smiled as she also sensed my nervousness and said "good-bye" to me as I was getting on my bike and riding off. I was so happy to see her smiling with me; instead of riding home right away that day, I wandered around town on my bicycle with all the beautiful thought in my mind. I enjoyed that afternoon in town, thinking about how I should start the conversation with her the next time.

Two days weekend was passed and not seeing her going to school those days seemed very long to me. The next school day, I went back to the bridge and wait for her after school again. When she came, I towed the bicycle by my side and walked to her. I said 'hello' and greeted her with a smile and this time she replied with the same manner. While we were walking side by side on the bridge, I could hear my heart was beating as a drum inside my chest. I silently took a few deep breaths to calm myself down so I could talk to her again, hoping that she would reply. After a silent moment, I took all my courage and started.

'What is your name?' I asked.

After a short moment of consideration, the moment seemed too long for me, she then said softly:
"Thuy, Ha Bich Thuy."

I was released from the anxious waiting period. Her full name means: Turquoise Blue River in Vietnamese. After hearing her full name, all of a sudden, the words just came out of my month: 'what a beautiful name!'

I did not know then that was her real name. We were walking on the bridge across the river, so I thought that she had made it up and did not want me to know her real name then; that was what other Vietnamese girls normally did. The Vietnamese idiom: "Son Thuy Huu Tinh" Sprang out in my mind. ('Son' means mountain, 'Thuy' means water, 'Huu' means exist or in existence, and 'Tinh' means love. The whole phrase means that: in a beautiful scenery of mountains and river there always exists love)

'My name is Son, Son Nguyen' I introduced myself.

She nodded her head gently with a soft

smile. I wanted to say something else, but I could not find word for my thought. We just walked by each other until we crossed the to the other side. I did not get on my bike as usual but still walked with her by her side. After a long walk, I then asked her again:

'Are you an An Phien student?'

She did not say anything, just smiled and nodded her head softly. I asked again:

'What year are you?'

"I am in senior year" She said very politely.

I wanted to keep on our conversation, so I said:

'I graduated from Ngo Quyen High last year.'

As I told her the school I had graduated from, I saw a slight expression of respect in her eyes.

Before entering into high school, students at that time also had to take admission test. It would depend on the test score of the admission exam that the student was arranged to a certain high school by the public school system. Ngo Quyen High was a renowned high school located right at the center of city and many students at the time wished that they would be admitted into this school. During the summer time before we took the admission test, students usually took private courses from the private instructors. The courses stressed those subjects that the students would take on their admission exam. I remember the summer before my admission exam, I had to come to the private math class almost everyday. During that school year, there was a student in my class whose house had a large room which was used as a private class room. His parents had organized a private class and had hired a good instructor to teach us at his home. There had been around twenty students coming each day then. A famous high school math teacher had been hired to teach us. He taught us how to solve all the math problems that might be in the coming examination that year. My mother had tried her best effort to have me in that class. But most of the students at that time would not have that same privilege.

As Thuy and I were passing by my home street, some of my neighbors were looking at us. I was shy but pretended that she was just an old friend that we had known each other previously and kept on walking normally. But Thuy was so shy that she walked much quicker. After we had passed my home street, she turned to me and said:
"Are you not going home?"
I looked at her and offered softly:
'May I give you a ride home?'
Thuy slowed down with her walking:
"No thanks; my house is very far from

here." She said as she shyly lowered her head down.

'Where do you live, Thuy?' I asked her again.

She said softly as she was trying to warn me not to follow her:

"Very far from here!"

'May I give you a ride?' I insisted.

"Thank you, but I get use to walking by myself" She replied.

I did not say anything but kept on walking quietly beside her. On her way home, she had to walk across a large open area close by Ngo Quyen High School. When we were on that street, I got on my bike and rode slowly by her right side.

The bicycle had an extra seat in the back. The North Vietnamese ladies at the time always sit sideway with both of their feet on the left side. All she had to do is holding on my back, lean her body and sit on the back seat of the bicycle. I then asked her again:

'Common, let me ride you home.'

She kept on walking but I sensed she was about to change her mind. I turned the front wheel of the bike and stopped the bike without getting down, blocking her way from walking forward, and warned her:

'Thuy, please sit on the bike and let me give you a ride. We are approaching my old school and the schooltime is just over. There

The First Love

are many people knowing me there. When someone comes out, if they see us walking together, they will tease us. So please, after we pass my school, you can get down if you want.'

My warning to her worked! She hesitated for a short moment, then held on the back of my seat and sat on the bike. Although she was sitting on the back of the bike and her weight added on the load of my bike, but I felt so much lighter and my heart was filled with joy. I started the bike and slowly rode her off through the street. When we passed the school, she did not ask me to stop the bike for her to get down. So I kept on biking and chatting with her, hoping that she would forget about getting off the bike.

As we were riding on the streets, I wished that her home was far away so we could ride with each other all that afternoon. We mainly talked about her school subject as we were riding with each other the first time. It was lucky for me that she did not ask me that day why I did not attend any college. I did not want her to know about our family history and also didn't want to lie to her either. It was a nice day and her house was far from her school so it allowed us more time together to acquaint each other. She now and then showed me the direction as we were riding through the different streets in town.

Her neighborhood was located deep inside the alley of the two large buildings at the outer skirt at the other side of the city. It surprised me to know that she was walking that far to go to school everyday. The alley to her house was very narrow that people normally would not ride in there but walk so that they would not bump into each other. When we got there, she asked me to stop the bike. We both got down, she thanked me for the ride. I asked if I could walk in with her to her house, but she refused my request. I guessed she was shy and afraid that some of her neighbor might see a stranger walking in with her. It was the first time we were together and I did not want to embarrass her. I said good bye to her and rode home.

On my way home that day, I was very happy and felt my old home town was so romantic; everyone in the neighborhood seemed so lovely. I knew that I could approach Don, my neighbor, and get him to pay for one night out at any restaurant as he had promised, but I did not even tell anybody about my first acquainting with Thuy; I tried to keep it as my secret. At home, only my mother seemed to know that something new had happened to me; I was happier than normal and often sang to myself.

The next school day, I came and waited to pick Thuy up at her school instead of at the bridge. We chose a different route to ride to her house so we did not have to pass over my neighborhood. It was a longer way to her house but we would have more time riding with each other. We became good friends since then.

Thuy was not just a pretty girl; I realized later on that she was intelligent, strong, and very kind too. She was the big sister in her family; she had one younger brother and two younger sisters. Both of her parents were working so she helped her parent to take care of her brother and sisters and helped them with their school works and the family chores. She did not have a lot of free time to go out with me. The most time we spent together was on her way home after her school and that was my most happy time in the whole day.

After we had known each other for a while, I remember one holiday, I came and picked her up at her house and took her to town. We were riding in the downtown area and when we passed by a flower booth at the central park, I attempted to buy her some flower, but she said she preferred to contemplate the natural growing flowers at the field than the already-cut-flowers. So I took her to Ha Lung Village (River Valley Village) at the countryside outside the city where people grew commercial flowers. We rode a long way to the village in a hot sunny day. She was sitting on my bike behind me and perhaps thought that I must be tired from biking under the hot sunlight. She took her Vietnamese style straw hat off her head and held it up behind me to cover my head while I was riding the bike. Her action touched me to the heart. The first time in my life I felt so important from what she was doing for me. I always thought that girls need to be protected from the torrid sunlight more than boy; however, my heart was filled with so much joy by her thoughtfulness that I wanted to be in that moment a little bit longer and did not say anything. I found a large tree by the road and stopped there to rest under the shade of the tree. After a while, we rode on another short road before we got to the out skirt of the village.

When we were there, I found a wide place with a lot of open space and put the bicycle down there so we could keep our eye on it. We both climbed up to a hill ahead and looked down to the village inside the area. The whole colorful plain ahead was filled with many fields of different kind of flowers. I had seen so many fresh flowers sold in town especially on the New Year Festival, but I had never come to the place where people grew so many different types them. That was the first time I saw so many different types of so many flowers in their natural uncut stages. The different color of each type of flower fields joined together as an enormous painting on the vast ground down ahead. The breeze over the fields of flowers brought a real pleasant air toward us. We sat down at the hillside next to each other to enjoy the spectacular view of nature. I slowly held her hand inside my hand. I could see her facial skin turned ruddier as she was blushing. I kept my hand so still for I was afraid that she might pull her hand back. I wanted to kiss her but very time I thought about it, my heart beat so hard that I could not make any move. We just enjoyed the peaceful view of the valley in silence for a long time with her hand so warm inside mine.

After we sat there for a while, she said that it was about time for her to be home. I wanted to stay there with her a little longer but I was afraid that she could get in trouble with her parents, so I rode her home. That was the first time we spent almost the whole day with each other and was one of mine unforgattable memories. After that time, I earned her trust and we became more close to each other. I once in a while visited her at her house and met with her parents. After knowing me, her parents seemed accepting our friendship and at times let us going out together to watch movie at night.

Our city had not had enough electricity for both the industrial and the residential uses then; therefore, the city had took turn to turn off the electricity of each residential area in town three to four days per week to reserve the power for the industry use. On those days without electricity, people had to use the kerosene-lamps at night in their homes. I used to hate the fact that the city had not provided us enough electricity to use. I sometimes read at nighttime but it was dark and uncomfortable reading by the flickering light of the kerosene lamp. Moreover, I was the one person responsible for buying the kerosene for my family. There was only one government store in the whole city that sold the kerosene at that time. Once every month, I had to carry a large plastic can and rode a long way to the selling place. When I got there, I also had to wait a long time for my turn to fill my can and then carried it all the way back home. But after having Thuy as a friend, the fact that the city not having enough electricity did not bother me anymore. Those nights when there were no street lights, the city became more romantic when we were side by side on the quiet street under the pure golden moon-light. We seemed closer to the nature and to each other without any artificial thing around us.

Our relationship at that age, which I didn't know how to define it, it was not just a

The First Love

normal friendship and I didn't know if it was of the serious formal lovers either, we were both still young at the time. But I had thought that it was the most beautiful and romantic boy-girl relationship of one's life. We never thought of or worried about our future together. Every time we were with each other, our minds were always at that very moment, and everything surrounded us became so beautiful and lovely.

17. The Second Escape

After knowing Thuy and our relationship were becoming closer with each other, daily life was also becoming sweeter and lovelier. We were together for almost a whole year and had many fond, pleasant memories with together. But the reality hit me one day when I was alone with my mother and she asked me:

"Young man, are you going to learn some trade for your future?"

I had never thought about that yet, I just kept quiet and did not reply my mother. I did not know what trade I could learn then. There was no guidance available for me. All my friends were in college and perhaps would obtain a job with the government after their graduations. But it was very hard to find work for someone like me, especially with my catholic family background. My brothers had been looking a long time for something to do and had not been able to obtain a job for themselves either. My second brother came home after his military service but had not had any formal job. To kill the boring time, he learned to play guitar classic with his friend. Everynight he just sat at home and practiced his guitar lessons. When I went home late at night; all people in our neighborhood had gone to bed and it was so quiet that I could hear the sound of the classic melody from his guitar at the end of the block. On the nights that the electricity in our area was cut off and my home street was dark, the guitar sound surrounded the old building in the dimly moon light made our neighborhood so peaceful but it was very sad too.

My second brother was in his late twentieth at time. After looking a long time and could not find any work to do, he was thinking about escaping Vietnam one more time. He talked to me and asked me if I want to escape with him. The last time when our family planned for the escape trip I was too young and not known about the planning until the last day. This time when my brother asked me if I want to go with him, I thought carefully about it. I did not want to leave my mother, I did not want to leave Thuy, the person I dearly loved, and I did not want to forever leave Vietnam with all my friends there. But I really wanted to have the opportunity to be abroad. I had always dreamed of traveling over the sea to some place. If refusing to go with him this time, I might never have another chance to do the same. That night at bedtime I thought about the planning trip and could not sleep. The first time I thought deeply about my future. The next day I told my brother that I would go with him if it is ok with our mother.

To leave Vietnam this time, we must find some fisherman that we knew and trusted, who were also planning to escape Vietnam. If the person trusted us, he would let us joint them, and we would pay for the trip with gold. However, we must keep our plan secretive within our close family members only. If the government found out, we would be jailed again. There was a person who my brother knew in the church. He was not a fisherman but his wife came from a fisher family. He also wanted to escape Vietnam and was planning for the escaping trip. He gathered a group of people who had money and wanted to escape with his family. He knew someone who he could buy a used boat from and was looking for a few more people to join him so he could have enough money to buy the boat. He approached my brother and mentioned the escape trip with him; my brother was just looking for that.

My brother came home and begged my mother for her permission and the money to pay for him and me. After our family's previous escaping failed, we had depleted our family saving. Also from the fail trip, we all knew the condition of people inside the boat and the risk of being arrested by the police. At first, my mother did not accept my brother's request. However, my third brother, although he was not planning to escape at that time, joined my second brother and tried to convince my mother. They mentioned about our family's dead end future and there was no other way out. After considering our request for a time, my mother wiped her tear and agreed to let my second brother and me go. She had a good old friend who she had known since the colonial time when they were both business partners. My mother borrowed some money from her and gathered enough money for my brother to pay for our trip. I kept the planning of our escape a secret and did not tell any of my friends, even Dzung and Thuy.

A few days before our departure, my mother called me in to sit by her and recommended me strongly on everything. She made sure that I had not let anyone know about the escape plan. My hair was long at that time and I did not look like a fisherman; she asked me to cut my hair and choose some old clothing to wear so I would look as a member of the fisherman's family while on-board. After all the recommendations, she asked me to take her to the cathedral with my bicycle. I did not know why she wanted to go to the church at the time when there was no mass, usually only my father did that when he was still alive, but I did not ask her for the reason, I just obeyed her command and took her to the church.

When we got to the church ground, it was in the afternoon and the whole area was very quiet. After locking my bike inside the gate area, I thought my mother would come to the church to pray, but she wanted me to follow her to the rectory area where the monks resided. When we were there, we met a young monk and my mother asked the monk for his help to inform the bishop that we would like to meet with him. The young monk led us upstairs into the guess room of the bishop and asked us to wait in there. I often came and played in the church ground of the cathedral but I had never been up here. The residing place of the bishop was solemn and kids were not allowed to play around this place. It was a large empty room with only a sofa table and two sofas at both sides. At the end of the table was a large pedestal setting against the wall with the large human-size statues on it. My mother and I followed the young monk into the room and waited, standing behind the sofas at the area close to the door to the inside area, while the young monk went inside to notify the bishop.

After a while, the young monk escorted the bishop out from the inside area. My mother and I both bowed our heads to greet the bishop, and the bishop smiled warmly as he also gently greeted us. He came to the area of the sofa table and asked us to come to the seat on the other side of the table. The young monk left us all alone in the room as the bishop was sitting down at the sofa on his side. We waited and also sat down on the sofa at our side after him as our etiquette.

The bishop was already at his high ages and did not perform regular Masses in the church except on the important holidays. I rarely saw him walking in the garden. Every time he had church affair and walked by us as we were playing around inside the church ground, we would always kneel down and bow our heads with great respect. I never saw his face in close distance until that time. That was the first time I sat so close to him. The bishop was a tall skinny man. He dressed in a red cassock and his short white hairs exposed under a tiny red hat on the top of his head. He had a straight high nose and his eyes were still very bright. He looked austere but his eyesight was warm and kind. I sat quietly next to my mother.

As she was starting her conversation with the bishop, I turned and looked close at the statues on the large pedestal behind me, suddenly, a feeling of shiver ran through my spine. The statue depicted a bare chess muscular Vietnamese soldier of the feudal period holding a big scimitar - a old weapon that looks half a sword and half a chopping knife - by both of his hands with a scowl in his eyes; his eyes glowered with the eyebrows rose high on his forehead. He was raising his scimitar to chop down to the nape behind the neck of a young man. In contrast to the fiery of the executing soldier, under his scimitar was a skinny innocent looking man, dressed in a black cassock, kneeling down on the ground. The young man holding his hands together in front of his chess, looking up onto the heaven such as he was praying peacefully. The statues looked so real and I was petrified seeing something so terrible in the office of a peaceful bishop. I did not know what the statues were about. I wanted to ask my mother then; however, the atmosphere in the room was quiet and solemn as my mother was talking about some serious matter with the bishop.

After a short conversation, my mother asked me to go to the corridor outside and waited for her. I realized then that my mother wanted to inform the bishop about my escape plan and asking him to bless us before my departure. I bowed my head, said good-bye to the bishop, and walked to the corridor. The corridor was a long and quiet place at the front area of the monk's rooms. I walked along the corridor and let my eyes wandered at the garden of the cathedral underneath for the last time. I thought that I might never see this beloved place again.

In about ten more minutes, my mother walked out and we went home. On the way home, I asked my mother about the statue in the bishop's guess room. My mother told me that the statue depicted the scenery of the execution of the first Vietnamese Martyr Andre Phu Yen who had died for his belief in the seventeen century. The Martyr died at the time he was only seventeen years old. When we were at home, she told me a lot more about the history of the Catholic Religion in Vietnam.

The night before my leaving, I went out with Thuy. She sat behind me on my bicycle as I rode her around our hometown. Somehow I felt confident that my escape would be successful this time. I wanted to take her to all those places that we had previously been with each other one last time. From my strange behavior that night, Thuy could feel something

The Second Escape

different was going on with me and asked me about it. I told her that I would be on a long trip out of town. She only thought that I would travel to some other city inside the country and asked me what city I would go to. At that moment I could not hold back and almost told her the true, but I remembered my promise with my mother and told her that I had to go to the South to learn a new trade. After a long ride with each other until very late that night, I took Thuy back to her house. On my way home, I felt sad for I could not tell her the true about what I was going to do. That was the last time I was with her. The next day, my brother and I escaped the country.

My Adventure to The New World

18. The Long Sea Journey

After being informed about the departure time, on the night of May 19, 1979, my brother and I prepared a small bag with just one set of clothes for each of us in it for our trip and left our home. That night the electricity of our area was turned off by the city. It was about 9pm and the streets were dark except for the vaporous moonlight. We came to the Tam Bac River and walked along the side of the river brink to the boarding site. I did not know where the boat was docked at but kept quiet and just followed my brother; we were not saying a word with each other while we walked hurriedly side by side under the ethereal moonlight. It took us about half an hour of fast walking before we got to the boarding site.

A sail-boat docked alone in a separated dark place by the bank of the river. As we were approaching the area, I took a quick glance around the whole area but I saw no sight of anybody; it was a very quiet night. When we were close to the location of the boat, someone inside the boat recognized we were coming and crawled out waving his hand to signal us down. A wood plank was already placed one side at the river bank and the other side on the boat. My brother got down onto the wood plank and walked to the boat. I followed him down and crawled into the boat behind my brother. Several people were already in there but it was dark inside and I could not see clearly who were there. I found an empty spot and lay down on the boat floor with our clothes bag as my pillow. Somehow I was not tremble with any excitement or fear as the last escape but felt at peace this time.

As I lay in there, I felt cozy and comfortable so I closed my eyes and just relaxed. We had to wait for all the people to come before the boat would depart. I fell into asleep and did not know how long I had slept until the boat started moving and wakened me up. I opened my eyes and saw many people either sitting or lying on the floor around me. The sails of the boat had not been raised by that time and the boat was moved slowly by someone wiggling a long paddle quietly in the water at one side of the boat. The long paddle was tied to the side of the boat at the handle section. That person was holding on the top of the paddle and wiggled the wider section gently in the water along the side of the boat. The boat moved slowly and quietly out from the spot and along the river.

When the boat was out to the open water, the sails were hoisted up. The boat moved gradually faster over the water surface but still slow. I looked out from inside of the boat through the opening; all I saw were two brown sails in the dim moonlight. The boat was still moving slowly, so I closed my eyes and tried to get back into my sleep again. I woke up a while later and realized it was already dawn-time and the boat was moving calmly in the Bai Tu Long of the Ha Long Bay with a decent speed. (Bai: attend upon, Tu: children, Long: dragon. The whole name means the place where the dragon's children attended upon their mother)

There were so many small islets rising out from the ocean water around the area. The boat was sailing smoothly over the blue tranquil water with all the islets around, concealing us from the sign of the border patrol guards.

With the daylight, I could sea clearly what

kind of sail-boat we were in this time. The boat was just an old river transporting boat which was normally used for transporting cargo over the river water way, perhaps it had belonged to some private family previously. It had not been built for deep sea fishing or ocean travelling. It was made by wood and bamboo and I was not sure of the boat's length but it was about twelve feet wide. The boat floor was constructed by wood planks which were spliced together over the large wood frame. Underneath the floor was the empty open space. The middle section of the boat had been constructed as a small living room and had been covered by the bamboo planks woven together as a rectangular sheet bending down at both sides of the boat. At two side of the boat over the woven bamboo sheet were the large bamboo bars, two on each side, which had been used to hold the bamboo plank roof down and also as the rails for people sitting on the curved roof. The boat had two sails, a large one in the middle and a smaller one at the front part of the boat.

There were many people on-board so the space inside the living area was reserved for women and children. Most of men would stay on the boat floor at the outside area. I preferred to sit at the outside area to feel the breeze of the bay area. When the sun started rising out in the horizon, I came up to the roof and sat there to contemplate the spectacular view of the bay with many islets of different sizes all around the whole region. The gentle breeze over the calm water created a magnificent and peaceful ocean view which is very unique to this region. Sitting on the roof of the boat at that moment, I felt as we were on a special sight seeing tour trip instead of the escaping voyage. The fisherman, the only person who knew the area well, was sitting at the rudder by the back of the boat. He was carefully steering the boat thought the interstice of the islets. Every time the boat passed close to a nearby islet, I was curious and tried to look upon the island to look for some animal living up there, but without binoculars, I only saw the plantation and some birds flying above the trees in the distance. We enjoyed our peaceful sailing for a couple of days inside the bay with the spectacular oceanic scenery.

The numbers of the islets were getting fewer and fewer as the boat was sailing out into the wide open water again. While day dreaming on the roof of the boat, suddenly, I heard someone shouted out "Get down, everybody get inside!"

The boat was coming close to the Vietnam-China Border. The fisherman told everyone on board that it was very likely that there are some border patrol canoe somewhere nearby. I got down and got inside the living area of the boat. The area was not large enough for everyone to hide in there; together with a few more other men, I had to crawl down the storage space underneath the boat floor through a square opening. Once we all got down inside that space, someone closed the opening by a large piece of wood plank behind us. I was squeezed into a tiny space with my back lying on another wood plank underneath and my face almost touches the upper boat floor.

Lying uncomfortably underneath the boat floor, I was smothered but trying to stay calm. After a while, I felt like I was suffocated. I kicked the boat floor and yelled 'Let me out, Let me out of here!'

My brother was sitting on the boat floor right at the spot on top me said quietly down to me:

"Just a moment, we are almost out of Vietnam Territory."

I had to take some more deep breaths and calmed myself down again. Another moment went by and I could not hold on any longer, I felt a sudden panic and kicked the boat floor harder and harder this time. Then a person above us removed the opening cover and pulled me out. Everyone else also got out from the underneath space. I felt released and looked out through the open area in the back of the boat, our boat was then already in the wide open ocean, there was not any sight of the island near our boat anymore. I followed my brother and another man, my brother's friend, to the outside area and got on the roof top of the boat. My brother pointed to the sight of an island in a very far distance behind our boat and said:

"We are out of the Vietnamese Territory. That is Hon Ngoc (Jade Island) of Vietnam."

I sat quietly on the roof area of the boat with my eye sight adhered to the misty view of the island until I realized that my face was wet with tear. I was looking at my beloved mother land for the last time. The sight of Jade Island was getting smaller and smaller until it disappeared out of sight. The boat was sailing deeper and deeper into the Chinese Territory. A mix emotion of both excitement and sadness filled my venturous spirit. I was happy for we were away from Vietnam Territory and out of the grip of the Vietnamese Police but was also sad that we might never be able to see our family and friends again.

The boat was sailing farther and farther from Vietnam. Suddenly we all saw the sight of a ship was approaching our boat from afar. The ship came closer and closer to our boat and then slowed down. When it got to a close enough for us to see it clearly, it turned out to be a large naval ship with guns on its top and many soldiers standing at the banister looking down at our boat. The war-ship stopped at a very short distance to our boat. One person in our boat who spoke some Cantonese Chinese talked to a formal dressed Chinese Naval Officer standing at the front banister near the bow. After they exchanged a few words, the officer asked another Chinese soldier to throw a rope to our boat for us to tie it to our front sail pole. Then the ship towed our boat slowly to a nearby port. At the port, another Chinese Officer ordered everyone out of the boat. We dock our boat, got out, and then followed the naval officer. Everyone had to walk down onto a rocky beach and followed the Chinese Officer to the Chinese Border Patrol Station of Fang Chen Port.

When we were still inside the boat, most of us had not affected by the waves and had felt comfortable. But when we walked down on the ground, many people then felt like having a seasickness and could not step firmly on the ground. Several people had to hold on one another while we walked on the rock beach as a group of drunken people following behind the Chinese Officer. We were ridiculed by the way we walked but no one dared to laugh; everyone was very nervous then.

At the border station, we reported to the Chinese Border Police the names of each person, the number of people on our boat (there were a few very young children on board), and the destination we were heading to. At that time, the Chinese and Vietnamese Governments were still in conflict with each other; therefore, after knowing that we were just some refugees trying to escape the Vietnamese Government and going to the Refugee Camp in Hong Kong, they released us. We all got back to the boat and continued on our journey.

After knowing that the Chinese Government would not capture or arrest us again, we decided to sail along the coastline close to land for safety. Our boat was an old sail-boat and people felt safer to sail close to land; in case there is a storm coming, sailing toward land would be much faster. While sailing along the coastline and every time we saw the sight of a small beach village, we would come in and stop somewhere at the beach to rest and asked the native for some fresh-water. As we came to those beach villages, the Chinese recognized our foreign boat right away. The Chinese sail-boats were different from the Vietnamese boats. Their boats were usually taller and had three sails, another small sail at the tail of their boat, one more than ours.

The beach village people often came out to meet us while our boat stopping at their place. People at those small beach villages were kind and truthful; they never rob anything from us, they just either traded with us or gave us some of their fresh water. There are many different ethnic groups of Chinese living along their coastline. Some of them don't even speak Cantonese or Mandarin Chinese dialects. We used gesture to communicate with those native that did not speak Cantonese. Our boat owner had prepared food and water for the trip; however, we wanted to reserve it for the later days and would trade for the fresh food from the Chinese fishermen from time to time. We took our watches or some personal items to exchange for their food, but for fresh water, most of the times they just gave us for free. Sailing close to the shore-line was slow and would take us much longer to get to our desired destination, but we were not in hurry, so we took time to enjoy our journey.

There were more than thirty people onboard and we treated one another as a large family member. We ate whatever we had, mainly rice and some pickled cabbage or dried fish. Our boat had a wood stove and we cooked our food at the back of the boat. Ocean water was used for cleaning purpose and we saved the freshwater for drinking and cooking only. The bathroom for us was just a piece of cloth tied by two sticks on both sides and stretched out at the rear end of the boat to hide from sight of people inside the boat. When someone needed to take a bath, that person would use a bucket to get the sea water from the ocean to use. Men kept wearing their underwear on while bathing and the women bathed with their cloths on. Most of the time I just waited for the time our boat was stopping near the shore and jumped down to the shallow water to take a bath down there. Sitting at the end of the boat to do the private activity while the boat was moving was a little scary. We had not brought much medicine with us; luckily, everyone was healthy and there was not any serious health problem with anyone on-board yet.

Living on-board was inconvenience for most people, but as a teenager, I really enjoyed the trip so far. Except for a little tired with eating almost the same food every meal, I loved the feeling of ridding over the wavy ocean surface. We were traveling during the summer season and the weather had been nice and without many raining days. I loved fishing and had wished that we had some fishing-rod to fish while on-board but there was none. Sometimes, I saw many fishes swimming near our boat but we had no mean to catch them. Once in a while there was a school of flying fishes flying above the ocean surface in a near distance, at that time we were hoping that some of the fishes would fly toward us and fall into our boat but it never happen either.

A time after we had travelled for days without seeing any other boat or beach village on our way and people were craving for some fresh food; finally, we saw a small Chinese boat near the beach and we approached it. After some greating manner with the owner of the strange boat, we asked the owner to trade his newly caught fish with a watch. The Chinese fisherman was so happy when we handed the watch to him. He gave us a large alive fish. The fish was used to make rice fish gruel. Everyone on-board had a good nutritious meal that day. After many days just eating the pickle cabbage, the fresh food tasted so delicious. I will never forget the taste of that so sweet and delicious fish soup that day. After we rested at that place for a night, we leaved that beach and sailed on again. And just as the other times, we would stop every now and then at those small fishing villages to rest, and spent many more days sailing along the coastline of the giant continent.

One time, there was not much wind at sea and the boat was moving too slow, so we came close to land and anchored our boat near the sand beach to rest and waited for favorable wind. That beach was a wild beach. After a few hours, the tide got down so low that our boat stuck on the sand floor at that beach. I and another boy, a couple of years younger than me, jumped out of the boat and went off into the beach-forest to get some dried wood for our cooking fire. That place was a wild area and must be far away from any village, there was no sign of any human living around. Close to the beach, the trees were small and it was hard to find any dried wood there. As we got deeper into the forest, the trees were getting bigger and higher. While in there, I was captivated by the different sounds of so many birds on the nearby trees. I looked up and saw many pretty and strange looking birds. Some of the birds twittered with pleasant sound as they were singing with one another. On the forest floor, some small wild animals were playing around the area. I went deeper and saw a family of animals looking like the dears feeding in near distance. Probably human had not come to this area to hunt; the animals were not afraid of us human yet and kept on feeding naturally.

After the other boy and I had gathered some dried woods, we went back to our boat. While we were walking back, the sound of a nearby young bird got my attention. I looked up and saw a small bird was fluttering its wings as it was calling to our attention. The bird had beautiful color on both sides of its wings and was perching at a low branch of a nearby tree. I handed the dried woods to the other boy and asked him to go back to the boat first. I turned around and came to the tree where the bird was perching. I walked softly and slowly behind the bird and the bird seemed not afraid that I was coming and didn't fly away. When I was very close to the bird, I carefully reached out to catch the it. As my hand was so close and almost got it, the bird flew away. However, the bird was a very young; it flew slow and perched at a low branch of another tree in a short distance. I followed the bird to that tree but when I was close to the bird and almost catch it, it flew again to another tree. I kept on trying to catch it a few more times, but the same thing happened again and again. It was like the little bird was playing game with me. I thought that it would be fun to have a bird on the boat to play with, so I tried to catch the bird again. The bird seemed tired and flew slower and with a shorter distance. I had caught young bird this way before and I knew that young bird would be tired soon and would not be able to fly anymore. So I chased it again and the bird flew away but weaker and descended inside a low bush. There was a small empty space in the middle of the bush. I thought the bird was trapped in there and would be caught easily. I slowly got inside the bush and looked for the bird, but I did not find it. It must be somewhere in there since I had not seen it flying out. I kept on looking but it was so weird that there was no sight of the bird anywhere. After searching for the bird for a while without success, I looked up and realized that it was getting too dark; I gave up looking for the bird and tried to run back to the boat but then realized that I had lost the sense direction. I stopped and felt panic. I looked around and ran again. After running for a long distance, I finally recognized that I was running in the wrong direction. It was getting darker and darker. I was tired! I turned around and ran back. After running for a while, I heard the sound of the ocean and then the very top part of the large sail pole of our boat appeared out from afar. The whole boat was gradually appeared in sight. It was a big released and happy feeling to see the boat still there.

When I came to the seaside, the tide had been up high and the boat was no longer laying on the sand floor but was floated on the water at a decent distance away. Fortunately people had not sailed on yet. I saw my brother and his friend Tuan were standing by the side of the boat looking very anxiously toward land. They both were happy when seeing me coming out of the woods. I waded in the shallow water and then had to swim to the boat; the water level was pretty high then. After getting on the boat, I was exhausted! I could not imagine what would happen to me if I was left behind alone on that wild place. People pulled up the anchor, the sails were hoisted up and the boat started sailing out to sea again. After the boat had sailed on our way, at times I still had goose pump on my body when a thought of being stuck at that wild beach and become a little Tarzan of the East came to mind (a cartoon movie I had watched during my childhood).

Since the beginning of our voyage, most of the time I had been a hilarious person, being excited by the experience of living freely out with the nature and travelling out over the vast ocean. But after the bird chasing incident, my energy level had depleted, perhaps from over panicking. I started feeling low of being in the doldrums and at times with a glancing sadness of being away from home. I was not as active as before and spending more time thinking about my mother and all my friends I had left behind. There were not many things to do on the boat. Sailing was mainly done by the helmsman and cooking was done by a group of women. Day by day, the men just sat having tea together and chatting with one another; sometimes they would play chess game, but I was not interested in those things.

Tuan, my brother's close friend, also travelled with us. Tuan and my brother were friends since high school and had been always staying by each other whenever they could. After high school, my brother had been compelled to joint the army, but Tuan had musical talent and had been accepted into Musical University. He had majored in violin and had also graduated by the time my brother was discharged from the army. I had known Tuan previously and liked the way he sang with the guitar every time he came to our home, but I had not known that Tuan was also escaping with us until we were on-board.

While on-board, Tuan and my brother were not interested in playing chess or chatting with the other men on the boat floor but just sitting alone, most of the time, at a separated place looking out to the wide ocean space. They both were young and romantic men, and often talked about their old friends or girl friends that they had left behind. I had not paid too much attention to them until this time. I came and sat with them, listened to their stories, and sometimes to Tuan's quiet singing. Tuan was a very talent singer, but he usually sang so quiet that I had to sit close to him so I could hear the lyric clearly. The lyric of some Vietnamese folk-songs made me missed Vietnam so much and sometimes drove me into tear. Had I not fought back the emotional feeling I would burst out crying at times.

One night the weather was nice and clear, the boat was moving calmly over the tranquil water and everyone was sleeping, except the helm person sitting quietly at the back by the side of the rudder with one hand on the handle of the rudder to control the boat. He was a former fisherman and was the main person responsible for stearing the boat. The former fisherman had a taciturn personality, rarely paid any attention to other people on the boat, and was the only person looking after the boat at nighttime.

That night I could not sleep so I got on the roof top of the boat and lay alone up there looking up the sky. It was a quiet night out at sea with only the vast darkness surrounding us. The stars at that time were so bright over the dark clear sky. I thought about our home and imagined my mother at home perhaps was not sleeping at the time and was worrying for our lives and wondering about my brother's and my whereabouts. I was deeply troubled by that thought. That was the first time on our journey I felt homesick severely. By then my mother must know that my brother and I had eluded the Vietnam Police's grasp and were drifting over the sea somewhere. I thought about her hard life and for the first time I was tormented by the nostalgia and a deep longing for her. I recollected all those stories of her childhood life that she had told me and thinking about how tough a life she had.

During her youth, my mother also had to follow her parents to evacuate her home village from time to time to avoid the mopping-up operations of the French soldiers. In her early childhood, she had a lovely and smart dog as her dear pet. One time her parents could not evacuate quick enough before the French soldiers got to her village and a French soldier came to her home. The soldier saw her cute dog and took the dog away. My mother was just a little girl at the time and loved the dog so much that she had grieved for many days after. When she grew up and by the time she was in her early teenage, she had to work very hard with her mother as a small trader and had often travelled along the Cai River (Mother River) without the accompanying of her mother. One time she was inside a sail-boat (perhaps as the one being used by us) and was travelling on the river with many other passengers. There was a young woman travelling on the boat with them. While on the boat, that woman was thirsty and used her hat to scoop up some river water and drank it. Normally the boat people had abstained themselves from doing that while travelling over the water; they thought that was a very bad omen. The boat owner saw that woman scooped up the river water but did not think she would drink it and could not stop her in time. A moment later, a large storm came along with heavy monsoon and the river water flew so harsh that the boat was turned over. Many passengers were swept away in the strong current. Fortunately, my mother was the only one saved by another small boat nearby and was spared by the accident. My mother strongly believed in praying, I remember she said that she had prayed Mother Mary before the comming of the storm and was saved that time. After my mother married my father, she had been the main person in the family taking care of most of the family business at home. My father had often been on the road with other business affairs then. After many years of hard work and when their business had earned some decent profit, they settled down with their own store. However, after they barely settled down with their business, just then the Colonial Administration ended. North Vietnam became Democratic Republic and the authority of the new administration dissolved their business. The new government had confiscated all their property and a lot of their saving. A few years living under the new administrative system, the whole family was back in tough life again. Then at the most difficult time under the new government, my father died and my mother became a widow when she was only in her fortieth. With a lot of effort and many years thrift, she had been able to save some money for the family. But again, we had been cheated by the corrupt authority cadre with all her saving and the whole family had been under the police detention for a while. Then her sons were scattered, one in prison and two were drifting over the sea somewhere unknown.

My face was wet with tear thinking about my mother and the difficult life she has been enduring. But I just let my emotion be natural and did not hold it back knowing that no one could see my face in the dark. Then I thought about my girl friend Thuy and my best friend Dzung. I knew that they must be looking for me and had probably come to my house to ask for my whereabouts. Overflow with nostalgia, I imagined the moment Tuan was also missing his girl friend and he sang his love song. The lyric of the song seemed echoing again in my mind:

> "I love an innocent girl
> She was so beautiful
> Her eyes were the stars
> Under the light of the moon
>
> Doted by her charm
> I sing many words
> Praising my dear love
> The most beauty of this world
>
> Where are you by now?
> My afflicted soul is searching
> Everynight in my dream
> Though you have not knowing
>
> Lookout to the waves
> I heard your sweet voice
> Singing from afar
> Amid the night without noise

> While lifting these words
> Those cozy nights
> Sitting by each other
> Appear out in sight
>
> Leaving you alone
> Without any word
> I felt the sharp pain
> Of our lives in this world.

The night went by so fast, perhaps someone inside the boat was waking up. The noise underneath drew me out of my imagination. The boat was still sailing calmly over the ocean surface. The dark sky was slowly turning into a dimly firmamen. Looking toward the horizon ahead, the pinkish sky was slowly appearing out in sight as dawn was arriving. People onboard started waking up to greet another fresh new day.

During the daytime, the ocean view had been beautiful and peaceful most of the time and the boat has sailed safely over the vast ocean surface. One time we saw a large beach village ahead of us and the village looked as a busy place so we came in. There were many large sail-boats docked around there. Many people were standing on their boats watching the other individuals playing some kind of boat maneuvering contest. We stopped our boat and docked close to their place. At one open area, there were many small sail-boats with only one man standing in the middle section of each boat holding the frame of a single sail of those boats. Those men stood firmly and controlled the direction of the sails to steer their boats on the water. It was not a windy day but those individuals could make their boats moved very fast over the water surface. They controlled their boats so skillful that even though their boats were moving fast and there were many of them but they would not bump into one another. They seemed having a lot fun, probably that was a kind of water sport of the native people there. They could sail the boats so easily such as someone was riding the bike on land. The other people standing on the large boats around the area were watching and cheering them. It was amazing and fun to watch their sailing skill. We watched them playing for a while and then decided to sail on our way again.

Sailing for a few more days and our food supply was running out so we were looking for another small beach village to trade for some more food. As soon as we saw the sign of a village from a distance, we turned our boat and headed to shore. This time, it turned out that was another busy beach town with many shops near the seaside. We docked our boat and some of us got out and walked on land. It was a good feeling that we were able to walk into that small town and visited many stores selling all kind of products on both sides of the narrow beach streets. I did not know the name of that town, but could not forget the scenery of that lovely beach-town and the busy narrow streets with many types of stores on both sides of the road. The people at that area spoke their unique dialect which we did not understand but they were nice native people. Be able to walk in a busy street for the first time after so many days sailing over the sea was a nice treat for all of us.

There were two brothers living in that town, after knowing our foreign boat from Vietnam was docked at their beach, they came to our boat to meet us. They probably came from a rich and well educated family. Both of them were tall, handsome men and dressed in finer clothing than most of the other people at that place. The two brothers were very polite and spoke well Cantonese Chinese dialect. One of the brothers gave us a few boxes of fine Double Happiness brand Chinese cigarettes. It had been a long time that people in our boat had not smoked a cigarette and our men were pleased with their gift. Every man was given some to try and really liked it. I was barely over eighteen years old then so I was also given one to try. Chinese cigarette tasted very different from what I had smoked before. It had the strange flavor of fresh flower but it was not bad at all. After talking with us and knew that we were on our way to Hong Kong, the Chinese brothers mentioned that they also had relatives living there and wanted to go with us. We did not know what to say to the two brothers right at that time and were discussing within our group about letting them go with us or not. Our people were afraid that the Chinese Government would found out and we could be in trouble; however, we did not say anything to the Chinese brothers then.

    Our boat owner had brought some rare herb from Vietnam and he gave some to the Chinese brothers as our return gift to them. The two brothers also gave us some Chinese money to spend at the shops in that beach town. The boat owner gave me some change. I took the money and went up onto that beach town while the two brothers were still chatting with our men in our boat. I bought some small and soft-cookie at the candy shop right by the beach. The cookie was similar the donut with a lot of sugar on it. As I took a bite of the cookie, wow! It was sweet and so delicious. I can not forget the taste of that cookie that day. After so many days over the ocean, my body was craving for some sweet. A simple cookie was a great reward for an undernourished body and it tasted so good. I recalled the time during the Vietnam War; some people in my hometown had carried a small bag of sugar down to the bunker with them during the air-raid hidings.

At that time I did not understand the reason for it and had thought that it was a funny and unnecessary thing to do. Having a cookie this time, I realized why people had carried sugar with them into the bunker instead of other dry provisions. I ate the cookie slowly as I walked back to our boat to prolong the enjoying moment with the sweet thing.

We left that village in the afternoon that day, and at the time we left that town, the Chinese brothers changed their mind and decided not to go with us. Perhaps they also realized the danger of escaping the Chinese Government and understood our people's concern by then. We untied the rope and slowly sailed our boat away from the dock. The two Chinese brothers, standing on the dock, waving their hands to us as our boat moving away from them. They looked unhappy and stood at the dock for a long time until our boat was far away and out of their sight.

Sailing along the coastline for a few more days, then we decided to sail straight overnight to Beihai Port, one of a large port in China. Instead of sailing along the coastline which would take us a few days, we could get to Beihai Port in just one night by sailing straight across the open ocean. That was the first time we sailed far away from land out to the open ocean. Everyone was a little anxious but also liked to test our sailing ability. We all heard about Beihai Port but no one has seen it before and were a little excited. We started out early in the afternoon and when nightfall the view of land was out of sight. Looked around was only the vast ocean water surrounding the boat. The boat was just small such as a tiny dot in the wide and dark space. There was no sight of any other boat anywhere. We were blanketed by the darkness of the night with only the bright stars above. Fortunately, the ocean was calm that night. That night, most of the men on-board did not sleep; a few of us were sitting on the roof of the boat looking anxiously forward for any sight of a fire-light of some other boat that might appear out from afar. At times I wondered if our boat was heading to the right direction; everywhere looked the same, just water. We were in the middle of the abyss. If any storm came at that time, our old sail-boat was too small and feeble in this vast water body and could be drowned in any moment. We all longed for the sunrise to arrive sooner, that night seemed very long.

Finally the dim sun light appeared out over the horizon. A while later, we saw the sight of one and then two other sail-boats coming out to sea. We were so happy seeing the sight of the other boats; we were no longer alone! After sailing for a couple more hours, the sun slowly and gradually appeared and we started seeing the sight of land far ahead. Everyone was up at that time and came out looking toward land. We steered the boat to shore and finally stopped near the port. There were some more sail-boats around the area but many were large ships berthing by the port.

Beihai Port was a large port in China. There were big cranes constructed on the port for loading cargoes in and out of the cargo ships. We looked onto the streets and saw some high buildings not to far away. There were security guards at the port and some Chinese Police standing on the streets. The Chinese at this place just minded their own business and were not very friendly or curious about our boat as the other native at those previous villages. Not feeling safe when we saw the police man standing nearby, we decided not to go on land to avoid getting into trouble with the security guards or the police. After resting at the port for only a short moment, we decided to sail our boat away from the port and stopped at another deserted place away from the city view.

After the first straight sailing was successfully which saved us a lot of time, we decided to sail in a straight line again from Beihai to Leizhou Peninsular. We departed from Beihai area early in the morning the next day and headed for Leizhou. That day we had favorable wind so the boat moved very fast. It was fun to sit at the front part of the boat to watch the boat cleaved the waves. The boat was pushed up and down by the waves in a rhythmic motion. I was sitting with two other boys right at the bow area to enjoy our roller coaster ride. We shout out with joy every time the tip of the boat rose up high and then dropped down as it passed each large wave. The boat sailed safely again until noontime and then the wind picked up and was getting stronger gradually. The sailor decided to lower the sails halfway down for safety. Even the sails were halfway down, the boat still moving too fast. The weather was changing and it seemed like a storm was on its way. We then decided to come closer to shore and sailed along the coastline again. The wind was getting stronger and the sky was getting darker. Fortunately, there was a small fishing village near Leizhou Peninsular; so we came in. There was a small bay at the base of the peninsular with many fishing boats berthing in there. The water in the bay was much calmer. We chose a spot right next too a large Chinese sail-boat and dropped the anchor there.

The Chinese fishermen on that boat were very friendly; they came out of their boat with a warm smile on their faces to greet us as we stopped our boat next to them. We also greeted them with a polite and respectful manner and expressed our appreciation for the shelter spot in their bay. The old fisherman had a small radio on his boat and knew ahead about the weather. After talking with him, we found out that there would be a big storm coming that night. We also learned from the old fisherman that there had been a few other Vietnamese sail-boats drowned previously at sea not too far from that area. We all felt lucky that we did make a right decision to come in and stopped in this village at the right time.

The old Chinese fisherman invited us to come to their boat. Their boat was a large sail-boat. The boat was made by thick wood planks nailed to the frame of large and strong beams. The room inside their boat was so much bigger than our and was arranged neatly as a living room of a small family. The old fisherman gave us some cooked sweet potatoes to eat while we were resting at their boat. The fisherman had only a young son with him on their boat that day. Probably they had a house on land and other members of their family were living up there. We did not ask them a lot about their family since our Cantonese was limited. The old fisherman was about sixty years old, had a harsh face but he looked frank and kind.

The fisherman said that the coming storm could be ninth-grade high (Chinese and Vietnamese measurement of the storm level) and could be very dangerous even our boat was inside the bay. After he saw our boat was too crowd with people and would be unsafe for all of us to sleep in our boat that night, he offered for all the women and children to come and sleep in his boat. He also asked his son, a strong young fisherman, to come to our boat to check all the safety situations in our boat.

The young fisherman was in his early thirtieth and was a mirthful man. He came to our boat checking for any possible unsafe area for the stormy condition. He kept a sweet smile on his face as he passed by anyone of us while checking around the boat. After checking for a while, he detected the rope we used for our anchor was not long enough. Since our Cantonese was not good enough to understand what he tried to explain, the young fisherman had to use gestures to explain to us that when the storm comes, our boat could be pulled down by the anchor and would be drowned if the wave was too high. We all were bewildered about the information but no one knew what to do then. The young Chinese man tried pulling the anchor up but it was stuck at the bottom of the bay. He did not hesitate but took off his shirt and bared his honey like color tanned skin and a burly chest. He jumped down to the water and dived down to bottom and pulled the anchor away from a large rock. From the length our anchor-rope we all knew that the water level in the bay was very deep; everyone in our boat stood around admiring his bravery and kind action. The young man came up after moving the anchor away from the rock and then pulled the anchor up. He then used another shorter rope from his boat and tied our boat tightly next to his boat.

That night, I slept at the storage area under the living room of their boat. I felt safe and secure lying next to the huge wood beams which exposed out at the inside space underneath their boat floor. I thought to myself: with these strong beams, this boat would stay intact no mater how big the wave is. That night, although it felt much more stable inside their boat than ours, I could still feel their boat was pushed up and down harshly by the strong waves. However, everyone was rested peacefully inside their boat without any incident. The next day, after the storm had passed, we thanked the Chinese fishermen and got back to our boat. They gave us some more sweet potatoes before we departed and continued on our journey.

We sailed peacefully for a couple more days and were getting close to the Qiongzhou Strait area. Qiongzhou Strait was made up by Leizhou Peninsular and the Hainan Island. It was in the evening and the boat was heading toward the strait; the waves were getting higher and higher as the boat was getting closer and closer to the strait area. By night-time, the boat came into the very rough sea area. The sky was clear and the moon was very bright that night. With the moon-light, I could see each wave as a colossal black-wall of sea water coming toward our boat. The huge walls of water were still getting higher and higher as our boat was getting closer and closer to the strait. After the last storm, that night was the first night on the journey I and many other people on-board were really intimidated by the ocean. We must pass this area to get through the strait; otherwise we had to sail around Hainan Island which is a much longer route. The boat would turn over easily had the helm person not steered the boat directly against each large wave. The waves pushed the boat up and down so hard that I had to hold my arms tightly onto the sail-pole at the front of the boat so I would not fell down to the ocean. Some other persons standing at the other outside areas also held on other parts of the boat. Only women and children were staying inside the living area. The helm person sat at the back of the boat with his hand holding firmly on the handle of rudder. Once in a while, he asked another person to hold the handle of the rudder for him so he could run up to adjust the sails so the boat would head in the right direction. The boat was pushed up and down violently but he was running back and forth bravely without any problem. We all prepared

My Adventure to The New World

and ready for anything might happen to the boat that night. Every time the boat was on top of the wave, I looked down to the water from the bow area but the surface of the ocean was so deep underneath that I could not see the ocean water; the tip of the boat was way up in the air. When the boat passed each wave, the next wave was coming. When the coming wave was getting close, the giant wall of black water was right next to us. I could stretch out my arm and touch the terrible wall of ocean water high above my head and right in front of me had I not so terrified that both my hands were holding tightly around the sail-pole at that time. The boat was raised up on top of the wave, and then dropped down onto the water surface as each wave passed through. The water splashed all over our bodies each time the front part of the boat hit down to the ocean surface. The sounds created by the boat hitting down onto the ocean surface was loud and very scary. I could not imagine what would happen if the strength of our old wooden boat could not sustain it from the force when it hitting down to the water underneath. The terrible sounds made one had a feeling that the boat might break apart at any moment.

Since the time I boarded this boat, I had not paid much attention to the helm person. To me, he had simply been a poor normal fisherman who also wanted to get out of Vietnam but had not had money for it. I had thought he had been lucky that the boat owner had let him travelling along with us without paying any money and sailing the boat has been his duty. He was around forty years old and was a quiet man. He was travelling with a teenage daughter and both of them rarely chatted with anyone on the boat hitherto. We city kids normally despised the usually poor and sometimes smelly fishermen when they came on to town. However, that night, while everyone was so scared, he was the only one running back and forth on the boat to adjust the sails and steered our boat through the turbulent water without showing any fear. The first time I deeply appreciated his presence. That night he seemed calm and strong as a brave captain in a perilous sea battle in some story I had heard of before and really admired him.

The boat had sailed many hours in the rough area but we were not out of the turbulent sea yet. I thought about my mother again. I was thinking about if we all drown in this place, my mother would never see or hear from us again. I remembered the story my mother had told me about the incident when she was young and was also travelling on a boat in the midst of a storm. She had prayed Mother Mary and was saved when her boat was turned over and drowned. I closed my eyes and started praying Mother Mary to help us getting through safely out of this raging water. As I was praying, the ocean was slowly calming down a little at a time and the wind also reduced its strength. The boat was not pushed up and down so hard anymore and then we slowly sailed into the QiongZhou Strait. The sun was rising gradually in the East. The water finally calmed down and daylight was arriving. We were in the strait.

The ocean surface inside the strait was totally different from the area we had just passed through. The waves seemed disappeared but there were many whirl-pools on the ocean surface appearing out here and there inside this area. With the bright daylight, I could see the water surface was sunk down much lower at the middle of each whirl-pool. Some whirl-pools were bigger than other. The helm person was cautious and very canny while steering the boat to avoid each whirl-pool as we sailed through this sea area. If the boat sailed too close to a large whirl-pool, it could be twisted around and might sink. At the time we were still in the previous rough sea area, I once had wondered why we had sailed through the dangerous area at night instead of during the daytime; seeing these whirl-pools, I then understood the reason our sailor had decided to sail through the turbulent sea area at night and arrived to this strait early in the morning. Without daylight, it would be impossible to sail through this strait. The boat was moving slowly inside the strait and we were very nervous as we watched our boat passing each whirl-pool. It took us a whole day before the boat passed through the strait area. When we passed the strait, it was getting dark and everybody was tired, especially the helm man, so we came to shore, stopped and rested for one night there.

Passing the Leizhou Peninsular was a major obstacle of the journey, the rest of the journey would be just similar to those previous peaceful days, that was what we all thought. We again took our time and sailed along the coastline not far from land for a few more days without any incident. Everyone again thought that we rather arriving Hong Kong late but safe than soon but too risky. It seemed no one on-board was worried about the dangerous of sailing at sea anymore after we had passed the most dangerous section. Although we were still concerned about our food supply, but we also knew that we could exchange our personal stuff with the native people along the coastline; the native living along the Chinese Coast were kind and very truthful anyway.

There was a couple in their late thirtieth who had come out from Saigon City and travelled along with us. The husband was born in Haiphong City and had moved with his parents to the South before our country was divided into two nations. After the country had been reunited again, he took his wife and a seven years old son back to visit his birth place. They had bought money with them while visiting Haiphong City and had decided to escape with us instead of going back home in the South. While on-board, he told us about many bad incidents which had happened to many other Vietnamese refugees in the South who had tried to escape the newly Vietnamese Administration by sailing through the Gulf of Thailand. There were many Thai pirates in that sea area. The pirates often carried guns on their boat and were very cruel. They would plunder the Vietnamese refugees when they saw their boats, had raped many women, and had even killed those husbands who had been trying to protect their wives. But sailing by the Chinese coastline was safe in that aspect; there was absolutely no pirate around this sea area.

It has been almost two months on-board since the time we departed from my hometown and all the clothes that I bought with me have been worn out from sitting everyday on the boat floor. There were holes in them but no one cared about our clothing condition then. We only cared about our sailing and concerned about having enough food and drinking water for everyone. There were not enough blankets for everybody on the boat; fortunately the weather was not too cold. However, I was getting weaker and weaker. I had not had any serious sea sickness and had thought that the longer the time we travelled, the more I would get use to it. But I had been wrong; I caught a cold by this time and started to have sea sickness and vomited frequently for a couple of days. I was just lying inside the living area with the assist of my brother.

After a few days just eating light rice soup I got well again. Early in the morning, I crawled to the outside area for some fresh sea breeze. It was another nice day out at sea. The weather was nice and clear with the cool breeze over the vast open space. It was nice to see the red sun gradually emerging out of the horizon again. Dawn at sea seemed so peaceful and was the most beautiful time of the day. Several people were sitting at the outside area chatting with one another, enjoying their tea and the early ocean scenery. We all thought that we had passed the biggest obstacle of the trip. Right at the moment we thought that the boat had passed the most dangerous section, the boat hit the aqueous rock that early morning and water was silently flowing into the boat. The boat was sinking and people on board were horrified by the incident. We had thought that we would all die at that wild place. The boat would had sunken all the way had we not recognized the situation soon enough. We were bare saved that day.

It was so lucky for us that the boat hit the aqueous rock during the daytime and it happened while it was moving not too fast. More than that, on that same day somehow Heaven had induced that one person was sitting right at the colliding spot at that very moment. By sitting there, he was able to hear the sound of the coming water to recognize soon enough what had happened to the boat. After a long struggling with the situation, the boat was pushed up on the sand floor at that wild beach. Everyone was exhausted after the accident but we all thanked Heaven that our lives were saved.

19. Arriving to Hong Kong

After everyone had rested for a while at that desert beach, together with some other men, I ran off into the wood and toward the mountain area. After we went pass a section of the dense woods and came close to the mountain range, there was a narrow open space between the two mountains. We ran along that narrow terrace and the area was getting wider and wider. Everyone was so delighted that we did not have to climb over the high mountain range. The terrace was ebbing into a flatter open area so we could run a little quicker toward land. From the high area looking down we saw a few boys playing in the distance. We were excited and called out loudly for them. The boys heard our call and ran toward us. When they were coming, they all looked surprisingly as they were looking at a few strangers from some remote planet. They did not speak Cantonese or Mandarin Chinese dialects which we might understand. They were talking with one another in a very strange tongue. We used Cantonese and tried to ask them for help but when the boys heard our Cantonese, they were ridiculed by the dialect and just giggled. We then had to use different gestures and tried to ask them to follow us to the boat. They seemed curious and followed us as we all walked back to the beach. When we all were at the beach, we leaded the kids to the bottom at the front part of the boat and showed them the cracked area.

After looking at the damage area, the kids understood what we were trying to explain to them. Two boys ran back to their village. The village must be far from our place since we did not see the sight of any housing. We just waited and did not follow them back, thinking that we could not speak their language anyway. After a long time, a native old man came out with the boys. After seeing the damage area of the boat, he got back to his place to get necessary materials and tools. The tide was getting very low and the whole boat lay on dry beach floor that afternoon. When the native man came back out, he bought a hand-saw, nails, some small wood planks, and some plaster. He was a fisherman himself and knew well how to fix the damage. The kind old man showed us how to fix our boat by using his gestures.

We were thankful and appreciated for the help and kindness of the native at that area. We camped at that beach for a couple of days to fix and to wait for the plaster to cure. Wood fire was used to speed up the curing process. After the damage area was well cured, we left that beach and went on with our journey again. From that day on, we sailed farther away from land to avoid any other aqueous rock in our path. There was not many boat or ship on our way through this whole sea section. Most of the time our boat was the only a tiny thing floating over the vast ocean space. Once in a few days, we would see the dim view of land in the far left. Instead of taking time enjoying our journey, we wanted to arrive to our destination sooner and did not want to stop at any place anymore. Sometimes the wind was against the direction of the boat, at that time we would sail the boat in a zigzag pattern in order to continue sailing forward. Fortunately, there was no storm during this whole time. We had been living for many days of out at sea; by then everyone on-board was almost exhausted.

For a long time without stopping at any place to replenish our food supply, the reserved food and drinking water were getting less and less. Each person was allowed to eat and drink only a minimum amount to survive. A few people had loosened their hope of being alive before reaching our final destination. From the time we left the Tam Bac River in our hometown hitherto, it has been more than two months without seeing any city lighting; people were desperated and really longed for some sight of a modern city (Two times our boat stopped at the places with possible city lighting, one time at a beach town and one time at a port city, but both times were during the daytime). It was only darkness at night and people on-board were hoping for some modern city life.

At the time people almost lost all their hope, one night while sailing out at the open sea, one person was standing at the prow saw a small brighter spot far ahead in the middle of the dark vaulted sky. He shouted out with joy: "Hong Kong! that is Hong Kong!", and pointing his hand to that area. Everyone came out and looked to that direction. We were filled with joy and hope again. We headed straight to that bright spot. After sailing for a few more hours, the brighter spot was gradually getting wider and wider over a larger area in the darkness. A few young persons were so excited that they kept jumping up and down with joy and did not sleep that whole night.

Arriving to Hong Kong

Very early the following morning, as the boat still heading in the same direction, there was a motor boat coming toward us from afar. The boat was moving very fast. We all thought the Hong Kong Coast Guard had detected our strange boat and came to check us out and our people were very anxious. In just a short moment, with its unusual high speed, that boat was already coming close to us. But it was not what we thought, the boat was a decent size motor boat and was raised high above the water with four staffs connected to two long sliding strips, one on each side of the boat. It was moving as it was flying in the air with those two strips on the surface of the ocean. That was the first time I saw that type of boat. Many passengers were standing at the outside by the rails of that boat looking at us. We all waved our hands at them but the boat just passed by us very fast. The only one person in our boat who had lived in Saigon City probabely knew about this type of boat and recognized the circumstance. He informed us that the flying boat was carrying its passengers from Hong Kong to Macao. At that moment, we all knew for sure that we were arriving to our destination.

When we came closer to Hong Kong bay area, there were a couple more motor boats of the Hong Kong fishermen coming out to sea. The people on those boats must had seen other refugee boats like our boat before, they seemed not too curious when they saw us coming in. The closer we came, the more boats we saw around the area. A moment later, as we were on our way coming near the harbor, I saw a little boy, only about ten years of age, sat at the cabin and controlled the steering wheel of a huge motor boat passing by us. His boat was veneered with shiny mahogany and looked luxurious. I was surprised to see such a young person could control a large beautiful motor boat. In North Vietnam at that time, all motor boats belonged to the government, made of steel, looked rusty, and only professional could control them, private fishermen in North Vietnam only had sail-boats then.

    Seeing the young boy controlling his huge family boat made me more excited about our coming new world. When we were near Hong Kong Harbor, there were a few more sail-boats around but many were large motor boats and cargo ships. The spectacular landscape view of mountains and sky-scraper slowly revealed ahead. Everyone on-board came out and looked toward the city. A Hong Kong Police canoe then came and stopped us from getting into the harbor. After talking to our people, they accorded our boat to a certain area of the harbor. At that time we had no more drinking water left on-board. They gave us some water bottles and some cookies and asked us to stop there and waited.

We escaped Vietnam at night on May 19 which was and still is a Vietnam holiday, and we had chosen that day since we thought that most of the Vietnam Police had been on their vacation. We finally arrived at Hong Kong in the morning on July 23. There were totally thirty seven people on-board. The boat owner was the oldest and he was in his fortieth at the time. The youngest was a little girl about three years old travelling with her dad. There was also a young couple and the wife was pregnant and almost due. It took us more than two months before we arrived to our desired destination. We all thanked Heaven that everyone was arrived safely to the new world.

Hong Kong is situated on China's south coast and is known for its beautiful modern skyscrapers standing behind the high cascade-mountain-view and in front of the deep blue bay. In contrast to the modern cityscape was to the view of some dark-brown-color sails of the ancient Chinese sail boats scattered at the harbor. We all were so happy while waiting at the harbor looking into the modern city right in front of us. Everyone was filled with hope and everything was so beautiful to us then. Looking toward the city from our boat at that time, I had a feeling that the landscape of Hong Kong Harbor that very first night was the most beautiful place I had ever seen hitherto. At night, the city lights from the skyscrapers lit up so brightly over a large area of the dark sky. The light reflected down on the black water surface of the harbor as the water surface was inlaid with so many sparkling stars. I had been in many places with magnificently natural beauty. But until then, the modern cityscape of Hong Kong was what I had only seen in the foreign movies. While standing there, I felt anxious and so excited; at times I thought that I was still in a dream. Not only me, everyone on-board seemed to have the same feeling too. We could not wait to be on land.

When we were still out at sea, people had worried for their lives and had been humble and getting along well with one another. However, after arriving to our destination and while waiting anxiously to get on land, some people seemed to forget about what had just happened to all of us. Being out at sea for a long time, we were like a bunch of wild people just came out of the jungle, stood waiting in front of the civilized modern world, a few men were prospecting about life in the modern world and what would happen to us after being on land. While in their excited mood, some men started boasting about their past and trying to show off their life experience and their 'broad understanding' of the new world.

Arriving to Hong Kong

There was a young man in our boat named Mui and he was only in his twentieth. He has been travelling with his daughter along with us; the little girl was the youngest person on-board. The beautiful girl was cute but she had probably missed her mother and had been crying a lot along the way. Mui had not known how to comfort his daughter when she was crying and had often beaten her. Most of us had felt sorry for the little girl and had not liked Mui much. While waiting at the harbor and was anxious for the Hong Kong Police to come and lead us on land, Mui also came out and stood by the side of the boat with other people to blather:

"If I am not with my daughter, I would jump down to the water and swim to land." Mui said to us.

Everyone standing around heard that and was worried that Mui might do something stupid and we all would get into trouble with the Hong Kong Police. Tuan was standing nearby and heard that too. Mui did not look as he was a person with good shape; he was short and looked a little chubby. Moreover, the distance from our location to land was pretty far. Tuan thought that Mui was just bragging. He was irritated by what Mui just said. He pointed to a large ship stopping at a much closer distance and challenged Mui:

"If you can swim to that ship over there and come back, I will give you one hundred dollar."

A hundred dollar bill was a big deal for us at that time and not many Vietnamese families had it. Everyone standby thought that Mui could not and would not do it.

"I would do that if I was not worry for my daughter" Mui replied:

People standing around was laughing when they heard Mui using his daughter as an excuse to back out from the challenge. Mui's face turned red.

"How about thirty laps around our boat?" he said to Tuan.

Tuan thought that Mui was just a bragging person and would back out again, he then said to Mui: "Go ahead if you dare."

Mui hesitated a little and people laughed again. Mui's face turned even redder, he then took off his shirt and jumped down to the water and swam.

No one had anticipated his action, everyone was surprised. More people came out and looked down to watch Mui and counted the number of lap he swam around the boat. After he had swum for two laps, he looked so tired and we all thought he would give up, but Mui kept on swimming. People stood worried that he would get exhaust and might drown and wished that he would stop. One person was looking for something to help him in case Mui want to climb up. But he did not stop. At times he looked as he was almost drowning and his swimming strokes looked awkward, but after he realized that more people, included the women, were out watching him, he got motivated and not giving up his swimming. After a moment of struggling, his body adjusted to the condition and he swam better and better. People standing on the boat were counting out loud the number of laps that he had finished. Finally he did finish all the thirty laps around the boat. He climbed on the boat and lay exhausted on the boat floor.

Tuan kept his word and took out the hundred dollar bill inside the pocket of his trousers and gave it to Mui. Tuan did not realize that even though he gave the money to Mui as he had promised and Mui did take the money, but Mui resented Tuan for his challenge and that would be the reason for what would happen to Tuan later on.

The next day, a Hong Kong Police canoe escorted another tiny Vietnamese refugee motor boat to our location and parked next to our boat. There were only four people on that boat. By talking with them, we found out that they had also escaped from the middle section of Vietnam (the region was in the former South Vietnam where the fishermen had motor boats) and had been luckily rescued by a cargo ship over the Pacific Ocean on its way to Hong Kong Harbor. After we waited there for another moment, the Police canoe came back and guided all of us to the dock. We were accorded to a temporary refugee camp right by the side of the harbor.

The camp had been temporary constructed and was administered by the United Nation. There were several water facets, about eight feet high, at the outside of the camp. We all looked tattered and dirty as we walked up on land. Before we were allowed to come inside the camp, the camp officials ordered all of us to come to the area with the water faucets and they sprayed our heads with the cleaning detergent and asked us to take a shower there. After the shower, they gave us some clothes to change and guided us to the camp.

There were already many other Vietnamese refugees had already arrived here before us and were staying inside the camp. The camp was a galvanized hut looked as a large close warehouse. There were two rows of metal bunk beds on each side of the warehouse. Everyone was assigned a bed to rest. My brother and I were assigned to stay together in one bed. In the middle between the two rows of beds was the large space wide enough for the lunch truck to drive in to dispense food at meal times. This camp was a close-camp; no one was allowed to go outside. Most of the refugee people did not carry any personal identity information with them; therefore, the time during our stay at this close camp was used for reporting our personal information to the United Nation Official and making new personal refugee cards.

The atmosphere at the Hong Kong beach was cool and comfortable. We were given some warm clothes and blankets while staying there. When meal times came, a lunch truck would drive through the gate into the middle section of the warehouse between the two bed-rows to give us food. The truck carried two huge metal containers, one contained steam rice and the other contained other hot comestibles. People were given a tray and got in line waiting for their foods. Two persons, standing by the food containers in the back of the truck, used the large ladles and dispensed food to each person in the line. People would take their foods back to their beds to eat. Although food was prepared in a large quantity, it actually tasted pretty good. After we finished our meals, we returned the empty trays back to the delivering truck. The truck would take all the dirty trays away.

Living in the close-camp was safe but was boring; we did not have anything to do. After a few days of alimentary food, I gradually felt healthier and more energized. As we were getting healthier, people with smoking habit coveted for cigarette. Someone staying in the camp somehow obtained some 555 brand cigarette and would trade for gold. A few people who had brought gold with them were willing to trade one once of gold for a carton of cigarette. Sometimes people shared one cigarette with many others; each person might only take one puff at a time. When it was someone's turn, that person would such deeply on the burning cigarette; with just a few turns, the whole cigarette would burn off and finished.

But the worst thing while staying at the close camp was the condition of the rest-room. There was a community rest room at the edge of the harbor which was constructed for the camp people. Either the children or the ignorant people living in the camp had used that rest room and really made a mess out of it. The first time I came there and saw it, I was disgusted so much that I never use the rest room the whole time during my stay. I just ate less and held back until I was released from the camp. It was very uncomfortable but I tried to cope with it.

After several days staying in there, I and a few other people travelling in our boat were sent to another camp by a bus. Sitting on the bus, I was so excited to see the city streets and the buildings as the bus drove through the streets. It was a cheerful feeling looking out from the bus window and observing the Hong Kong people and all the buildings around us. Hong Kong was so modernized compared to North Vietnam. The streets were crowded with so many modern cars running fast on the roads, much faster than I had ever seen in Vietnam before. There were so many advertising signs with Chinese characters and English hanging all over on the buildings at both sides of each street. The pedestrians were weaving hurriedly along the sidewalks. They also walked much faster comparing to people in North Vietnam. I did not see many bicycles on the streets as in my hometown, many people in Hong Kong were riding on the two-level buses instead. Everything around us seemed strange and very new to me.

After driving through many busy streets in about thirty minutes, the bus came to an old three story brick building. There was a big sign hanging at the open gate: JUBILEE REFUGEE CAMP. After driving through the gate and a long driveway, the bus stopped at the front yard of the camp and we all got down. There were many other refugees had come here before us and were living in this camp. A camp official came out to meet us and informed us about our new temporary residence.

20. The Refugee Camps

Tuan together with my brother and I were allowed to stay in the same small room on the third floor with another young family who arrived here before us. As an idiom, we all often heard that "the earth is round and soon or later we will see our old friend again" and it seemed true; it turned out that the man of the family we would stay with was an old friend of our family back in Vietnam. We were so surprised and very happy to meet each other in this new place. He was a Chinese National named Tien and was one of my oldest brother's best friends. He had come here with his wife and their two boys about a year before us. At the time he was still in Vietnam, he usually came and stayed at our house. There was time he had worked with my brother in our family business at our place and had even lived with us in our home for months. I called him brother Tien, regarded him as a big brother and had many good memories about him. He could speak both Chinese and Vietnamese and was a very energetic, tall cheerful man and always kept a smile on his face. I recall the time I was a small but very active boy and had wanted to grow tall as some of my friends, Mr. Tien had often showed me the necessary exercises to do at our home in his spare times. He had loved to smoke the Lao tobacco of my father after each lunch and had had a very unusual habit of arranging his resting place before his smoking. I had always been ridiculed by the way he preparing the place to take a nap right after having the tobacco at our home. Since the floor of our house was impeccably clean, he would set a pillow down on the floor right in the middle of the living room even there was more comfortable beds available in our house. After preparing his resting place, he would get back to the tea table, sitting at the chair next to my father's special tobacco pot. He would prepare the tobacco into the pot deliberately and slowly before firing it. After taking a few short breaths and burned the tobacco gradually, he would take a deep and long breath of the smoke to burn off the tobacco. After that he would hold most of the smoke inside his lung and very slowly lay down on the floor with his head on the pillow. Then he closed his glassy eyes very slowly while blowing out the smoke in his lung. In just a few minutes after that, I could hear his loud snoring right in the middle of the house. I must walk with gentle and quietly steps around him. A few times by accident I tripped and stumbled on him while he was sleeping and woke him up, but that did not make him changing his favorite resting place.

I had not seen Mr. Tien for a long time. The last time I met him in our home, he was still a single man, but after he and my brother stopped working together at our family business, I had not seen him since. When the Vietnamese government boycotted the Chinese Nationals in Vietnam, he left Vietnam with his family and also came to Hong Kong and was staying at this camp. This time we met each other, brother Tien had already become a married man and lived with his wife, a nice Vietnamese lady. They had two sons, five-year old and three-year old boys. I were very glad to see that he did not change much and was still healthy and happy as he used to be after so many years, and all his family members were with him here.

After getting out of the close camp, we all felt comfortable as we were able to walk freely on land again after so many long days living in a small boat out at sea without knowing what our future would be. Moreover, we were in Hong Kong! A modern city that I had only heard about before. A place that would have been appearing only in my dream had I not taken the escaping trip. That was a huge turning-point of my life. Right after putting away my personal stuff into the room, I got down to the ground level and walked around to know more about my new place and checked out for any one staying in this camp that I might knew previously.

The Jubilee Refugee Camp was an open-camp and people living in this camp could go out to work; the refugees called this camp a free-camp. It was an old and decent three-story brick building with a rectangular shape and was located right by the side of the ocean. The building was built on a strong concrete foundation by the side of the harbor. The fence at the backside of the camp was at the edge of the bay with the sea water right at the base of the building foundation. There were many small compartments inside the building; people living in the camp could come in and out from both sides of the building. This building had probably been built as a hotel before it was bought by the United Nation to use for the refugees. This was the most secured refugee camp in Hong Kong, or so it seemed. People lived in separate rooms and we could lock our rooms at night from the inside before bedtime. There were also several bath-rooms on each floor which made it pretty convenient with the personal cleaning for the residing people here.

The building had a small convenient store at a corner in the first floor. In the front of the store was a community area constructed with some simple galvanized metal sheets next to the fence. Inside the area, a color television set was mounted high on the wall in front of a few benches and was left on most of the time. During the day time, there were always several children sitting at those benches to watch the daily shows on TV. It was a happy feeling seeing the kids behaving naturally and happily inside this camp. They seemed remembering by heart the song of each show and they recited loudly the songs along with the TV before each episode. From time to time, the TV would show some long Chinese fiction martial art movies and most the boys in the camp loved it. It only showed a few episodes each day and the rest of the time was used for commercial advertising. By that time, color TV was not available in North Vietam. It was here that I first saw those Chinese martial art movies that I had heard or read about in some similar fiction novel and I really enjoyed watching those movies too. Sometimes the old black-and-white Charlie Chaplin Comedies were televised; at that time the area would be crowd with so many people standing around the area to watch the show. During those moments I could hear the sound of people laughing from a far distance.

The very first night at this new camp, my brother and I together with Tuan were taking a walk inside the camp around the building to enjoy our freedom and the cool ocean breeze in the area. It was about ten o'clock and the surround area of the building was very quiet. We were just relaxing as we strolling slowly side by side under the dim lights inside the courtyard in the cool atmosphere of the bay area. As we walked into a darker area, suddenly three guys jumped out from a corner inside the building and surrounded us. Their faces were covered with back cloths except the spots of their eyes. Each one of them was holding a big Chinese kitchen chopping knife in their hands. We were all petrified and scared. One of them spoke Vietnamese and asked Tuan to take off his jean and gave to him. Tuan flinched a little but then took off his jean and handed it to that guy. Tuan was left with only his under wear on him. Right at that moment I thought that they would ask my brother and me to do the same, but another guy only asked me to take off my small gold ring, about one once of gold, in my finger which my mother had given me before my escaping trip. After I gave the ring to him, they took the stuff and all of them immediately disappeared into the darkness at the stair-base area of the building. Everything happened so fast. We stood in disbelief for a while before we regained our calmness and walked back to our room.

When I was back to our room, I wondered why those robbers only took Tuan's jean but not of my brother's and mine. It seemed that they knew my brother and I did not have anything else with us except that small ring in my finger. I found out later from my brother that Tuan was from a family with good financial status. His mother was a gold-smith in Vietnam and she had given him some gold and valuable jades together with some US money before his escaping trip. He had kept all of those stuffs with him inside the pockets of his jean. The robbers took his jean and he lost everything. I wondered why the robbers had known so well that Tuan had had those stuffs with him in his jean since the robbers had not done the same to us.

Tuan reported the incident to the Hong Kong Police the next day. It took the police a few months to trace the stuffs from the Hong Kong jewelry stores to find out who had sold the jewelries to them and caught those criminals. But by that time, the robbers had already spent all the money from selling most of those stuffs. Tuan only got a few of his jewelry items back.

I did not know and was not bothered

to find out what the police would do to those guys. I just knew that they were the Chinese Nationals who had lived in the same city with us in Vietnam and had come here before us. They had been considered by the people of our neighborhood as the street trouble makers at the time they were still in Vietnam. They had left Vietnam early with their families after the relation between China and Vietnam getting tensed and had come here long before us. Mui, the guy had travelled on the same boat with us, perhaps had been one of them at the time he was in Vietnam. Someone in that group knew Mui. After winning the swimming challenge and obtaining a hundred-dollar-bill from Tuan, Mui realized that Tuan had more money and many other jewelry and had carried those stuffs with him in his jean. Although Mui had won the challenge, he resented Tuan for that. As Mui was also transferred to this camp on the same day with us, he informed those robbers about Tuan's possession right after our arrival. Those robbers had planned to rob Tuan right away the first night before Tuan could find a place to hide those. My brother and I just happened to be with Tuan that night.

As most of the other boat people, after the robbing incident, we had no money left with us to buy anything here for ourselves. However, the United Nation provided the new comers with meals everyday in the paper boxes. In Hong Kong, some restaurants prepared meals and put those in a special rectangular paper box. They put steamed rice at the bottom and either barbecue pork or chicken on top of the steamed rice. The United Nation ordered meals from them and the restaurants would deliver the meal boxes to the camp. At mealtime, the new comers would come down to the United Nation Office at the first floor to obtain our meals. Each person had one box for each meal.

Although the free meals were tasty, I had not been able to eat on the first couple of days at this camp since I was having a serious problem with constipation and it was very uncomfortable. It was the result of many days staying in the temporary close-camp and had not used the rest-room there because of its condition. Fortunately, the camp also had a small clinic and a doctor had to insert some kind of small medical equipment into my body to cure the problem. After that I could eat again and got ready to find a job to support myself. We also needed some decent clothing for any possible job interview; luckily, the United Nation also had one room of used garments which were donated to the camp through goodwill from many people around the world previously. The camp official let all the new comers came in and chose some clothes for us to use.

The room I stayed in was a small room with enough space for only two bunk beds. My brother and I slept on the lower level of one bed. Tuan slept at the upper level of the same bed. The other bed was used for Mr. Tien's family; Mr. Tien and his wife slept at the lower level and his two sons slept on the upper level of that bed. Each room at the second and third floor of the building had a separated balcony. Standing at the balcony in my room looking out was the peaceful view of a portion of the Hong Kong Island with mountains behind the sky-scrapers and in front of the deep blue bay water. We was fortunate that our room was located at one of the best location behind the building with the open view of the ocean.

The first several days at the camp, I spent a lot of time at the community area at the ground level to get acquainting with some people and be familiar with the new place. Mr. Tien gave me some Hong Kong money to spend at the camp store. I bought some chewing gum and a cup of coke at the store to try them out. That was the first time I ever had some coke; it tasted very different from what I had drunk before but I really enjoying it the very first time. I also liked to watch the legendary Chinese martial art movies and the Charlie Chaplin comedies showed on the television at the community area and spending my time with the kids to learn to speak some Chinese.

The Refugee Camps

It was a new world and everything was new and interesting to me.

From watching the commercial programs on TV, I started to realize that almost anything was available in Hong Kong and anyone could buy those products as long as one had money; it was very much different from North Vietnam where so many things was in real shortage then. I was happy and excited. But after a while when I was somewhat settled down, I started to have homesickness again. Every time I compared the life of people living Hong Kong with the people in Vietnam, I felt for the Vietnamese people and it brought me back to my family there. During my childhood, perhaps except for guns and ammunition, Vietnamese people had been living for a long time with war and were in deprivation with almost everything else. Sometimes late at night when the camp was quiet, I sat alone at the balcony of my room and looked out to the sea. I missed Vietnam so much; I missed my mother and my family. I thought about all my friends and could not imagine until what time I would be able to see them again. When I was with them, I never thought about how important their presences were to me; after losing them, I then realized how much I had need them around me and was really tormented by a deep longing to them. Some nights sitting alone at night in the balcony looking out to sea, I murmured

My Adventure to The New World

some lyric of the Vietnamese songs that I had listened to so many times at home. These songs had been played many times from the tape that my brother had bought out from Saigon City after 1975. Many songs were written by Trinh Cong Son a well known South Vietnamese song writer. Most of the songs were about the miserable circumstances of the people living in the war zone. At the time I was in Vietnam and listening to these songs, I had somewhat understood the meaning of the lyric but did not feel much the emotion the song writer had put into his songs. But at the camp, when I hummed the song to myself, I then felt the meaning of each word that the author had implied in them. One night while sitting alone late at night by our balcony looking toward the direction of my homeland, I heard a Vietnamese song from someone playing his cassette-tape-recorder in the camp. I thought that person must having the same feeling as I had at that moment. The lyric of the song resounded in the quiet night and I could hear it clearly:

> " The tear for a child
> The mother was glad her child asleep
> The tear for the river
> Nurtures the moss and weeds
> The tear for the land
> Has long been exhausted
> The tear for the people
> The people of unfortunate lot

The tear for the clouds
Sleeping high above the forest
The tear for all the trees
Tilting over the hill without rest
The tear for the man
The body had dried of blood
The tear for my country
Why still flowing without stop?

Oh! The stream of tear
Has flowed so many years
Flowing so many years
Longing for someone so dear
Oh! The tear in my heart
Flowing into my soul
Calling me amid the nights

The tear for the bird
Had left the forest
The tear for the nights
The nights without rest
The tear for my love
Our land is in ravage
And the unnamed tears
Please help me to manage.

I had heard this song from my brother tape-recorder before, but at that time I had not felt the song much. Hearing this song in the camp away from home, each word of the lyric seemed to penetrate into my agitated heart.

After the song was over, I realized my face was wet with tear. That night I could not sleep at all.

All the refugees living in the camp were from Vietnam. There were Chinese Nationals, mainly from North Vietnam, and the Vietnamese from different regions of the country. Many of them had left Vietnam and had come here long before us. Some of them had been in the camp for more than a year. Once in a while, the bus brought some more new Vietnamese refugees to this camp. Most of Vietnamese were fishermen that came from the middle region of Vietnam, some from the North. I rarely met anyone from Saigon City or people from the southern regions; most southerners used other routes and came to Thailand or other countries near their regions. Adult people living in this camp were working except for those who had small children and had to look after them inside the camp. I did not work at the time so I hung around the camp and spent a lot of time with Mr. Tien's boys to learn and to practice my Chinese speaking with them.

After I had learned and spoke some Chinese, I followed a Chinese National, who I recently acquainted and was also living in the camp, to his work place and applied for the same job he had. He worked for small galvanizing factory on fifth floor of an old commercial building in a remote area of Kowloon Peninsula Region. I was hired by the owner of the factory and started working right the next day. Everyday I woke up very early in the morning and walked to the bus stop near the camp waiting for my bus. When the right bus arrived, I would get on the two-level-bus to the work place. It would take the bus forty five minutes to get to the factory. Sitting on the bus was an enjoyable time for me as I could observe many different areas of Hong Kong City. Even when the first level was empty, I always sat on the second level of the bus so I could see farther view from the bus window.

The streets of Hong Kong were so crown with so many kinds of vehicles during busy hours and traffic jams happened almost every time it was raining. I sometimes got to the factory late due to the traffic problem, but the owner of the factory was a nice man and he would comprehend the situation. The owner had been a refugee himself as he had come here from the mainland China previously. He was in his late fiftieth and had owned the galvanizing family business for a while. He rented the whole fifth floor level of this commercial building as the manufacturing site for his business. There were only eight people - included myself, the guy who introduced me to this factory, and six other Hong Kong Chinese - worked for him. The owner treated us all as the members of a family which made me felt very comfortable although I didn't speak Chinese very well and it was the first time I in my life I had a formal job.

At lunch time, the business owner ordered food for everyone working in the factory from some place nearby, and he would eat with us too. Sometimes I looked down from the opening at the stair area of the building during our lunch break, I could see the lunch delivery guy coming in with two piles of containers on both sides of his bicycle. He had all the dishes in two large aluminum containers with different layer for each dish and tied them together into two piles at both side on the back of his bicycle. When he arrived at the building, he left his bicycle at the first floor and carried the two piles of containers up for us. The dishes were still hot as we all ate together on the floor, included the owner, in the stair area right out side the door of the factory. After we fished, we left the empty dishes at the door and the delivery guy would come back to take them away. I did not know where the owner had ordered our lunch from; the building was at an industrial area and I did not see any restaurant around. But the comestibles were very well cooked and I loved the way they prepared all the dishes. I had lived in Hong Kong for almost two years, but I never had any other dishes similar to those.

A few weeks after I found my job, my brother also found a job for himself as a machine operator for a sub-branch of San Miguel Brewery.

I was so excited when I had my first pay check in my hand. Since the price of cigarette was the first consumable product I knew at the time, I calculated the amount of money I made in one day was enough for me to buy a whole carton of a 555 brand cigarette in Hong Kong that time. I recalled the time while we were staying in the close-camp, someone had traded one ounce of gold for it. I also compared the money I just made with the salary of a normal worker in North Vietnam then; to have the enough amount of money to buy a carton of the same cigarette in North Vietnam at that time, a normal Vietnamese worker had to work for a whole month. I remembered when I was in Vietnam; most people only had enough money to buy a couple of cigarettes at a time from the peddlers in the black market.

After having the first pay check, my brother and I went to town to buy our new shoes and clothing. I did not forget to buy some stamps so we could send letter back to Vietnam. Life after having a job was much busier and keeping me away from my nostalgia. We often went to the theaters not far from our camp to watch movies at night. At only one corner of a city block, there were two theaters next to each other which showed many different kinds of movies everyday. The area was always crowded with a lot of people, especially at night. At that time, I liked the Hong Kong martial art fighting movies the most and often watched those; those kinds of movies were not available in North Vietnam then. I had heard about Bruce Lee, the famous Chinese movie star, and had always wanted to watch his movies previously but was not able to see any of his movies until that time.

     Eating out at the small restaurants by the streets for the common working class people was enjoyable for me. It was convenient and not expensive, but the food quality was not bad at all. The restaurants usually located right by the sidewalk and foods were cooked at the open area right in front of the customers. My Chinese speaking skill was very bad then, but eating at those places we would not need to speak good Chinese to order the dishes. We just had to point to the comestibles placing in front of us and the chef would understand what we wanted and he would cook the ordered dish right in front of us. We just sat and enjoyed watching the chef cooking the dish until he finished and brought it to our table for us to eat while the food was still very hot.

The Refugee Camps

We could buy raw foods and cooked them in the camp too. There were two community kitchens, one on each side of the building on the first floor. Some people brought their stuff down there to cook; however, it was not very convenient as we had to bring our kitchen utensils down there each time. My brother and I were not very good at cooking either; therefore, most of the time we just ate at those inexpensive restaurants. We only stayed in Hong Kong temporarily and didn't have to pay for anything except our food and clothing, so the money my brother and I made was enough for us to live comfortable while we were there.

In general, life of the Vietnamese refugees in Hong Kong was much better than many other refugee camps at some other countries around Vietnam. However, many refugees staying in here were from both the south and north regions of Vietnam. Especially, it was right after the Vietnam War and there were still some people in both the North and the South misunderstanding and detesting each other. There were totally six refugee camps in Hong Kong, not included the close-camp. While staying in this Jubilee Camp, I heard that there were some tussle happening among the refugees at other camps. However, most of the people involved in those serious fights were either the ignorant young men or the former trouble makers from both the north and south regions. They sometimes even fought with one another among their own groups too.

After living in the Jubilee Camp for a couple of months, I followed a few other young people and joined them in a Christian activity group for the refugees at the nearby Baptist Church and learned English there. We were allowed to use a small quarter of the church as class-rooms for our English lessons. The teachers were the volunteers who organized the classes for us. There were three teachers for the whole group: Bob Piper, a young and ebullient man about thirty years old from the United States, Dennis Ross, a hilarious young lady around the same age with Bob Piper was from England, and Mrs Ramona, my teacher and she was from London. There were about thirty of us and I was the only one from North Vietnam, all other students were from different regions of formal South Vietnam. The volunteer teachers were enthusiastic and cheerful individuals who created a fun and lovely atmosphere at every class night for the group. We were provided books with simple English daily conversations to use for our lessons. The whole group was divided into three separated small classes. I was in a class with a few other people at my age and our teacher was the elegant English lady. She was my first English teacher, in her fortieth and was from London. She was not an excite person as Bob and Dennis but very sweet. We all loved her and called her Mrs. Ramona. Once in a while, Mrs. Ramona would take the whole class out on a picnic trip with her on the weekend to have the out door group activities together.

The six refugee free-camps in Hong Kong at that time were: Jubilee Camp, Sam Sui Po Camp, Kai Tak North Camp, Kai Tak East Camp, Akai Lau Kai III, and Akai Lau Kai IV. The refugees living in one free-camp often visited their friends at other free-camps in the weekends or holidays. Kai Tak North and Kai Tak East camps were the largest and were right next to each other, only separated by a fence. These two camps was far from where I stayed but most of the people I knew were staying at these camps and I often went to visit them there. There was a large community room at Kai Tak East camps for catholic people to celebrate Mass on every Sunday. At the Lunar New Year Festival, I would come to these camps to celebrate our New Year with my friends as we had usually done in Vietnam.

Although living in Hong Kong after having a job was materially comfortable, but like everyone else in the camp, I wanted to settle down permanently in some place as soon as possible. Once in a while, the Delegation of a nation from the Free-World, through humanity, would come to the camp to interview the refugees. If the refugee or the refugee family wanted to settle down at their country, they would sign up for the interview with the Delegation, and if they were accepted by the Delegation Official at the interview, they would prepare and wait for their flights to the permanent residing places.

Tuan had a younger sister who had left Vietnam previously and had settled down in Canada for a few years. When the Canadian delegation came to the camp, Tuan signed up to interview with the Canadian Delegation. He was accepted by the Canadian Delegation right after the interview and would fight to Canada sometime in the near future. My brother and I had no relative living in any of those nations at that time and we also wanted to come and live in Canada with Tuan; therefore, we had signed up to interview with the Canadian Delegation; however, we were not accepted by the Canadian Delegation after the interview. My brother was very depressed after the Canadian Delegation refusing us. He was sad for not able to live in the same country with his best friend. We did not know what country would ever accept us and felt disheartened, but there was nothing we could do except waiting.

A few weeks after we interviewed with the Canadian Delegation, the United Stated Delegation came to the camp. My brother and

I wanted to live in America since it is next to Canada, but we were from North Vietnam, a former enemy of the United State, the United State Delegation would not accept us, so we thought. But we found out later that the United State Delegation would interview any refugee that had been refused by another country previously; therefore, it turned out that we were fortunate that the Canadian Delegation had refused us and having the opportunity to interview with the United State Delegation. Although we did not have much hope that the United States Delegation would accept us but signed up for the interview anyway.

On the interview day, my brother and I came to the office of the United Nation on the first floor of the camp. We came into the small empty room and I saw a frigid face American Officer with and a Vietnamese translator sitting in their chairs on one side of an old rectangular wood table. I had only seen some picture of the fallen American pilot on the Vietnamese news paper before, that day was the first time I saw a real American in person and I was a little nervous. There were two empty chairs set at the other side of the table and we were asked by the serious looking American Officer to sit down at those chairs. The American officer introduced himself and asked us a few questions regarding our family history and the reasons why we had left Vietnam. We just answered those questions with honesty. As the translator translated our answers back to the American, I noticed his facial expression was not changing a bit. I felt hopeless! However, after we told him about our religion, the American Officer asked us for a sign that we were genuine Catholics. Simultaneously and without telling each other, both my brother and I made the sign of the Cross over our heads in front of him. As there was an invisible power, right after we did that, his facial expression changed and he looked much warmer with sympathy. Finally, he asked us to take off our shirt to check for any tattoo on our bodies. After he saw no tattoo on us, he politely thanked us for interviewing with him but did neither refuse nor accept us at the time.

After the interview and from the change in the American Officer facial expression, we felt that there might be hope for us to come and live in America. So my brother wrote a letter and asked a person who knew English to help us with the English translation. We sent that letter to the American Consulate in Hong Kong. A few weeks later, we received a reply letter from the American Consulate accepting us to come to the United States of America. What a joyful moment when we received their letter. I felt a big relief when a new country accepted us. More than that, we would be living in one of the most powerful nation of the world

The Refugee Camps

that I had never before dared to think about.

There were more new refugees coming to Hong Kong after us and the United Nation needed rooms for the new comers at the Jubilee Camp. Therefore, after staying at this camp for a few months, my brother and I were transferred to Sam Sui Po Camp located very close to Jubilee Camp. Sam Sui Po Camp, as many other free-camps, was bigger than Jubilee Camp and all people living in this new camp were working and able to support themselves. The camp was constructed within a whole block, extended close to the side walks of the streets, and was fenced around with galvanized metal sheets. There were many galvanized huts inside the camp ground. Each hut was set up with two rows of bunk beds on both sides. There was one common hut with separated smaller individual shower areas with high water faucets (there was no hot water in all the camps in Hong Kong). There was no common kitchen here as in Jubilee Camp, cooking was done by each individual at the outside of the hut under the extension of the roof. Some people arranged their own places at the outside of their huts and cooked foods to sale for people living inside the camp. It was here that I was first able to try different dishes cooked by people from different regions of the South Vietnam and I really enjoyed them.

Living in the new camp was not as safe as at the Jubilee Camp since there were too many people living inside the same hut. The bunk beds were close with each other and sometimes conflict happened between some young men. One time I witnessed a serious fight between two young men at the open area by the side of the camp ground. As I was walking to the area to do my routine exercise, I saw one small guy was holding a big kitchen chopping knife and was chasing another taller guy. When the tall guy was stopped by the fence, the small guy with the knife jumped to him and used the knife to attach the tall guy with many blows. The tall guy fell on the floor and his blood spilled out all over the ground. Some other people shouted out for help as the small guy ran off. The injured person was brought to the hospital after the fight and no one knew what happened to him after that. That was the one serious incident that I knew during my stay at that camp.

After I was transferred to the new camp, I also found a new job at a hand-bag factory located a lot closer than the previous one. Instead of riding the bus for forty five minutes each way to the work place, it only took me twenty minutes walking to the new place. The company I worked for was a big company that made leather hand bags and shipped them all over the world. I worked at one of its two separated factories located on the seven floor of a high commercial building right in town. Not as the old building of my previous job, this building was new and modernized, had elevator instead of only stairs. Most of the people worked at this whole building dressed nice and clean.

When I first started working here, my job was to operate the leather cutting machine. After a while, the company needed someone in packaging area, so I was moved to the new area and worked in the packaging department. After working in the packaging department for a few months, I was again transferred to work as an assistant for the engineer of the company. With this new job, I was often allowed to travel with the company engineer back and forth from our location and the company main head quarter at another location. I really enjoyed this new position since it was a good chance for me to see more new places and learned more about life of the people living in Hong Kong.

Also by working at the new place, I found a small Catholic Church in the area with Mass celebrating in Vietnamese language. I went to that church to attend Mass every Sunday. In this small chapel I met a very special and interesting priest who had helped guiding me spiritually in the beginning of my new and strange world. The priest was also a Vietnamese and we called him Father Minh. He was in his fiftieth, looked modest and was an indulgent man. He organized and celebrated Mass in a small chapel in the second floor of a large building in Vietnamese language for the Vietnamese refugees living nearby. His affability made us felt comfortable and close around him.

I usually came to the chapel early when there was either no body or just one or two persons in the chapel before Mass-time. The priest often came to the chapel early for the Mass preparation and I assisted him with some light chores from time to time. I found out that Father Minh was born in Hanoi and had served in South Vietnam before 1954. After Vietnam had been divided into two separate regions under two different administrations, he had remained living and serving in the South. He had also travelled to the United State and many other foreign countries before. He had been aboard during the fall of the South Vietnam in 1975 and had not come back to Vietnam after that. Father Minh was a erudite person. I didn't ask him about his permanent residence but he was not living in Hong Kong as a refugee at the time.

Many of us refugees attending Mass at the chapel were going to settle down in America as our final destinations and were curious about our future residing places. We all wanted to know more about life in the United States so we usually asked Father Minh a lot of questions. One time after Mass, some of us were spending time around the priest and we were talking with him about life of the other Vietnamese who had left Vietnam before us and had settled down permanently in the United States. I recall the priest recommended us at that time:

"Living in America, you all should be careful otherwise you could lose your own faith!"

I was surprised by what he just said. I had always thought that America is a free nation and no one there would force anyone out of their faith. I had even thought that the American were the spiritual people. At that time I recalled that my mother had once told me that : "Not like the atheistic people in our government who believe that God does not exist and there is no deity influence in our human life, the American people are the people with strong faith. They are way ahead of us and their technology was so highly developed that they were already able to reach the moon, but they are still very humble that they had printed 'In God We Trust' in all the bills of their paper money."

I wondered about what the priest just said and asked him:

'Father, we came from a country with a government that did not like any religion; although they had not yet forbidden the citizens from religious practice, but it seemed to me that they did not like us either. However, even living in that environment, I had never thought that we would lose our faith. Now that we are coming to a country which is free and even favors religious belief, why should we have to be cautious?'

The priest smiled and said slowly:

"It is hard to eliminate the faith of someone by external force; however, faith can be easily changed internally."

After talking with the priest that day, I kept thinking about what the priest said to us. I recalled what he warned us about was also one of the concerns that my mother had recommended me the day before I left her but I was not paying too much attention to it then.

Although the living condition at the refugee camp was fine and it was an opportunity for us to meet many kind and loving people, many of us were tortured by the nostalgia from time to time. I was young at the time and often felt homesick and powerless. For that, sometimes I felt like to do something harmful to myself. I needed some advice from a mature adults to guide me with my immature thoughts. Meeting with Mrs. Ramona, my English teacher, and Father Minh at this place was a big comfort for me and I had learned a lot from these individuals. One time I came to church and sat with the priest after Mass, I asked him:

'Father, last time you said that our faith can change internally, but I still don't understand what you mean?'

Father Minh didn't say anything, he just nodded his head gently. I was impatient, so I said to him:

'Father, I may still be young but I think my thinking is old and I want to know more about this subject.'

The priest looked straight into my eyes and said kindly:

"How do you know what old people think when you said that your thinking is old?" and then he looked away.

His response roused me. 'How can I see someone's thought?' I realized in a whim that I was too arrogant. I lowered my voice and begged him:

'Please explain for me why I should be cautious about my faith after coming to America?'

He slowly turned around and said:

"Living in Vietnam, there was not too many opportunity for you to work or achieve materially; therefore, you might have a lot of free time and went to church more often and would spend more time for our religious activities; however, when you come to America, you will have more opportunity to work and probably will achieve more with your material life. Therefore, you will spend more time working and also more time enjoying the success of your material life. Moreover, seeing many people around you were also successful, you will be afraid of getting behind and will spend more time working to compete with them materially. Day in and day out with a new life style, things will change. You know that the Vietnamese people often say that "gan muc thi den, gan den thi sang" (near ink will be dark, near light will be bright). When you spend less time with your spiritual life, it will slowly wither. If something changed very slowly, you might not notice and recognize it until it was too late.

That was the last time I talked with him. I was transferred to a new camp for the preparation of my final trip to the United States. The new camp was too far away from that chapel and I could not go back there to attend Mass anymore. At that time we did not have cellular phone and I lost my contact with him since. I really regarded priest Minh as my mentor and very thankful for all his advices as they equipped me in my new life journey. While living in the refugee camps, I was curious and very anxious about my future in the United States. At the new camp, sometimes my English teacher, Mrs. Ramona, came to visit me and I wished that could speak better English so I can ask her about her life in England too.

The new camp was called Akai Lau Kai III and was the last camp I stayed during my time in Hong Kong. Akai Lau Kai III was also constructed similar to all other refugee camps in Hong Kong except the Jubilee Camp. It had several galvanized metal huts inside a close fenced area. All people staying in this camp were preparing for their flights to the final destinations. I had to quit my job and also stopped learning English from the Baptist church because this camp was too far from the previous location. Mrs. Ramona was so kind as she often came to the new camp to visit me and helped me with my English conversation skill.

Since we were no longer working, my brother and I, joined with two other men, took turn to cook our daily meals at the outside of the hut. There was a girl staying at the bed close to our. She was a Chinese National from North Vietnam and spoke Cantonese fluently. Every morning, she walked to the market to buy food back to cook at the camp. I was the youngest in our group and was assigned to buy food for someone else in our group to cook. Everyday I carried a plastic basket and walked with the Chinese National neighbor to the market to buy food for our group. She knew the market well and was very familiar with the way people selling their stuffs in the market. It was fun walking to the market with her. She once in a while educated me about how to cook some special Chinese dishes and what food it was good for our body. I enjoyed our conversation but I did not like to cook much. At the market, I only needed to choose the products and she would always bargain for the best prices. When I bought the stuff back to the camp, someone else would be responsible for the cooking.

Living in the refugee camp was not very safe even in this very temporary camp and we were glad that we were finally leaving this whole place. All people in this camp would stay here for only a short time before we would flight to our permanent destination. Unfortunately, there were still some tussles happened to some persons right before their flights. I beheld two bad fighting incidents right in my hut.

The first time was one young man fighting with a group of other men at his bed. The man was holding a big cooking knife in one of his hand and standing on the second level of his bunk bed. On the ground around the bed were four or five other young men with different kind of weapons, some with a knife, and some with a piece of wood in their hands. The men on the ground were trying to attack the young man on his bed. But the man on the bed showed no fear and chopped down from his bed without any hesitation to anyone getting close to the bed. After the men on the floor tried a few times and could not touch the man on the bed, they all left. As I was watching them fighting, I was so worry for any of them. I felt released as the men on the floor left our hut and no body was injured; however, I did not know if they would fight again later.

Another fight was happening at night during our sleep. I was wakened up in the middle of the night by the terrible crying of someone near my bed. When I woke up, I realized that someone else had used a big cooking knife and chopped down at that person while he was sleeping in his bed. This young man was a different man that I had seen from the previous fight. He perhaps had involved in a fight previously and the guy he fought with took revenge while he was sleeping. He was injured seriously and was taken to the hospital. I felt sorry for the injured man who must had gone through so many obstacles before arriving here but had foolishly involved into the conflict with other people to such a serious extend and be injured right before his final destination. I did not know what would happen to him after that incident.

After staying in Akai Lau Kai III for about more than a month, my brother and I with several other people in that camp were provided the necessary documents and were guided to a special bus parking at the gate of the camp. The bus took us to Hong Kong Air Port. We boarded a Boeing 747 airplane and flew to San Francisco.

Dear Readers,

Thank you for selecting my book! This is the first book that I wrote and it has not been edited thoroughly. A friend of mine, while reading my story, had helped me fixing some of the mistakes in my writing. I corrected them and uploaded the new e-book edition in my personal website (riverbreezepublishing.com). I also added an epilogue and acknowledgement sections in the digital edition. Please check it out when you have some time. Again, thank you very much for your encouragement and support.

Sincerely,

Paul Nguyen

RIVER BREEZE PUBLISHING

QUICK ORDER FORM

Email orders: orders@riverbreezepublishing.com
(Please send us an email to confirm our current address)
Mail orders: 15080 SW Bangy rd. Lake Oswego, OR.97035.

Please send the following books. I understand that I may return any of them for a full refund - for any reason, no questions asked.

_____

_____

_____

Name::_____

Address:_____

City:_____State:_____Zip:_____

Telephone:_____

Email Adress:_____

Shipping by Air:
U.S. $4.00 for first book ans $2.00 for each additional product.
International: $9.00 for first book and $5.00 for each additional product (estimate)

Cut along this line